THE

REVELATION

A GUIDE TO HELP IN THE STUDY OF REVELATION

EVANGELIST DAN GOODWIN

**Printed in the USA by FBC Publications and Printing
Fort Pierce, FL 34982
www.fbcpublications.com**

TABLE OF CONTENTS

INTRODUCTION	3
DANIEL Chapter 9	7
TRIBULATION TIMELINE CHART	10
REVELATION Chapter 1 ----- CHRIST AND HIS CHURCH	11
REVELATION CHAPTER 2 and 3 ----- THE SEVEN CHURCHES	15
REVELATION Chapter 4 ----- THE RAPTURE	24
REVELATION Chapter 5 ----- THE SEVEN SEALED BOOK	27
REVELATION Chapter 6 ----- THE FOUR HORSEMEN	32
REVELATION CHAPTER 7 ----- SEALED one hundred forty-four thousand	36
REVELATION Chapter 8 ----- A PAUSE IN HEAVEN	39
REVELATION Chapter 9 ----- HELL ON EARTH	41
REVELATION Chapter 10 ----- JESUS AND THE LITTLE BOOK	44
REVELATION Chapter 11 ----- THE TWO WITNESSES	47
REVELATION Chapter 12 ----- THREE WONDERS IN HEAVEN	50
REVELATION Chapter 13 ----- SATAN'S UNHOLY TRINITY	53
REVELATION Chapter 14 ----- one hundred forty-four thousand WITH THE GOSPEL	57
REVELATION Chapter 15 ----- SEVEN LAST PLAGUES REVEALED	60
REVELATION Chapter 16 ----- SEVEN VIALS OF GOD'S WRATH	63
REVELATION Chapter 17 ----- FALL OF RELIGIOUS BABYLON	66
REVELATION Chapter 18 ----- FALL OF POLITICAL BABYLON	69
REVELATION Chapter 19 ----- SECOND COMING OF CHRIST	71
REVELATION CHAPTER 20 ----- GREAT WHITE THRONE JUDGMENT	73
REVELATION CHAPTER 21 ----- NEW HEAVEN AND EARTH	76
REVELATION CHAPTER 22 ----- GOD'S FINAL PLEA TO COME	79
A LESSON ON WHO CAN GET SAVED DURING TRIBULATION AND WHEN	81
CAN A PERSON BE 100% CERTAIN OF HEAVEN	82

· **All Scriptures are from the King James Bible and are in *italics*.**

INTRODUCTION

To the average Christian, the book of Revelation is a closed book. Though everyone seems fascinated by the teachings of it, most are either too afraid of it or have been told all their life that it is too hard for the common man to comprehend. My friend, nothing could be further from the truth! The book of Revelation is no harder to understand than any other book of the Bible, but it does take some study. God is the author of the book; He will guide you into an understanding of it if you will let Him. Notice also what it says in Revelation 1:3 *"Blessed is he that readeth, and they that hear the words of this prophecy, and keep those things which are written therein: for the time is at hand."*

God promises a special blessing to those who read, hear, and keep the things written in Revelation. **To read** means just that, read the book of Revelation. **To hear** means to read with understanding, to think about what you are reading, to read wanting to learn truth. **To keep** means to obey the things you learn from it. So you see, the blessing is not to the casual reader, but to the one who reads with a desire to learn truth and with a heart of obedience to that truth. I have just given you a Bible principle that will help you understand not only Revelation, but any book of the Bible. Why not decide before beginning this study that you mean to "keep" this three point outline to the best of your ability? Decide you are going to READ the Bible with purpose, seriousness, and a commitment to OBEY what you learn. That is what the Psalmist meant in Psalm 39:3 *"My heart was hot within me, while I was musing the fire burned: then spake I with my tongue...."* That is what Joshua 1:8 is saying: *"This book of the law shall not depart out of thy mouth; but thou shalt meditate therein day and night, that thou mayest observe to do according to all that is written therein: for then thou shalt make thy way prosperous, and then thou shalt have good success."* The Bible is not a book for the casual reader, it is a book to be read, a book to be studied, a book to muse and meditate upon, a book to be loved, respected, and obeyed to the letter. Then and only then will it open up to you and bless you beyond measure. The Word of God can be a fire in your bones as it was to Jeremiah. Jeremiah 20:9 *"Then I said, I will not make mention of him, nor speak any more in his name. But his word was in mine heart as a burning fire shut up in my bones, and I was weary with forbearing, and I could not stay."*

The purpose of this study guide is to give a basic chapter by chapter outline, rather than a verse by verse study, which would be much too lengthy. Each chapter will give you a major theme, a summary of the chapter, along with some lessons and personal application. It is my desire that this study guide will be a simple and helpful tool in your study of Revelation.

PROBLEMS WITH INTERPRETATION
(Why there are so many different interpretations of the Revelation)

1. Many are hindered by faulty teaching from their past.
2. By not discerning the literal from the symbolic, many misinterpret the book.

For example, Revelation 1:7 is to be taken literally because the context does not lead us to look at it as symbolic. *Revelation 1:7 "Behold, he cometh with clouds; and every eye shall see him, and they also which pierced him: and all kindreds of the earth shall wail because of him. Even so, Amen."* In contrast, *Revelation 1:14 "His head and his hairs were white like wool, as white as snow; and his eyes were as a flame of fire...."* this verse is symbolic because it says "like wool" and "as a flame." The context of the scripture will help you discern whether it is literal or symbolic.

3. One of the biggest reasons for a faulty interpretation of the book of Revelation is a lack of understanding of parenthetical chapters. By parenthetical, I mean a chapter inserted to explain something that has happened in the past, something that is coming in the future, or to further explain the present. It is like using a parenthesis in a sentence, only it is a whole passage or chapter instead of a few words. Let me give an example of this principle in some Scriptures:

1 Peter 3:21 *"The like figure whereunto even baptism doth also now save us <u>(not the putting away of the filth of the flesh, but the answer of a good conscience toward God,)</u> by the resurrection of Jesus Christ...."* Do you see the parenthesis used here? The sentence would make a complete thought without the words in parenthesis, but makes more sense with those words included. See also *Revelation 2:9 "I know thy works, and tribulation, and poverty, <u>(but thou art rich)</u> and I know the blasphemy of them which say they are Jews, and are not, but are the synagogue of Satan."*

The book of Revelation is in order, but there are a number of "parenthetical chapters" inserted that will throw you off if you do not understand what they are. For instance, Chapter 7 is inserted between the sixth and seventh seals as a parenthetical chapter to explain some things. It is NOT in order, but explains future events. As we go through the outline, I will let you know which chapters are parenthetical, but basically, they are chapters 7, 10,11,12,13, and 14, although there are some parts of these chapters that are not.

<u>Now let's look at some basic facts about the book of Revelation:</u>

1. The human author is the Apostle John. John the beloved. The one *"whom Jesus loveth."* He was exiled on the island of Patmos for preaching Christ (Rev 1:9). As you study the lives of the great men God used in the Bible, as well as those being used throughout history, you will find they were men that were going against the flow, and were at war with the world's system. They used to say of Brother Lester Roloff, "You're rubbing the cat the wrong way." To which he replied, "Well, turn the cat around then!" Persecution from the world is part of living for Christ. Friend, are you at peace or at war with this world?

2. Revelation means to uncover, to unveil, as a sculptor would pull the sheet off his work of art for the audience. Remember, it is the unveiling of Jesus Christ, not

John! See Revelation 1:1 *"The Revelation of Jesus Christ, which God gave unto him, to shew unto his servants things which must shortly come to pass; and he sent and signified it by his angel unto his servant John...."* The book of Revelation literally shows us a side of Christ that we do not see in the Gospels. In the Gospels we see him born in a lowly manger and riding on a donkey. In Revelation, we see him as King of Kings and Lord of Lords coming on a white horse with power and majesty and might! He came bringing mercy the first time, he is coming back the second time with wrath. The Psalmist certainly knew more than we realize when he said in Psalm 2:12 *"Kiss the Son, lest he be angry, and ye perish from the way, when his wrath is kindled but a little. Blessed are all they that put their trust in him."*

Friend, you must fall upon Him for mercy now, or one day He will fall upon you and grind you to powder. See what Jesus said in Matthew 21:44 *"And whosoever shall fall on this stone shall be broken: but on whomsoever it shall fall, it will grind him to powder."*

Revelation shows you a side of Christ that Hollywood won't show you, and sad to say, most churches won't preach to you.

3. The book was written around A.D. 96

4. The theme of the book is the Revelation, or the unveiling, the making known of Christ.

One who does not know the Christ of Revelation well, does not know Christ well.

5. The key verse and also the basic outline of the book is Revelation 1:19
I. Chapter 1 .... Things which thou hast seen.
II. Chapter 2 - 3 .... Things which are in John's day.
III. Chapter 4 - 22.... Things which shall be hereafter.

6. A More detailed outline of the book is as follows:
I. Chapter 1: Introduction - Christ and his relationship to His church
II. Chapter 2 - 3: The Seven Churches - The Church Age
III. Chapter 4: Rapture
IV. Chapter 5: Seven-Sealed Book
V. Chapter 6 - 19: Seven Year Tribulation Period. (Daniel's seventieth Week - Daniel 9:22-27)
VI. Chapter 20 - 22: One thousand-year Reign, Great White Throne Judgment, New Jerusalem

7. Take everything literally unless the passage indicates it is symbolic.
This is very important to the understanding of Scripture. Words such as *"Like as,"* or *"as of a"*, indicate that the passage is symbolic not literal.
EXAMPLE: Revelation 1:14 *"His head and his hairs were white like wool, as white as snow; and his eyes were as a flame of fire...."* His hair was not "wool," but "white like wool." His eyes were not "fire," but bright "as a flame of fire." You will see this all through the entire book of Revelation.

8. Why God uses symbolisms to teach truth:
1. Symbolisms are timeless. They have the same meaning and application in every

generation. For example, a candlestick is used to represent the church in Chapters 1 - 3 as well as the two witnesses in Chapter 11. The candlestick is a type of light today just as it was in generations past. It is a timeless illustration or "type," it means the same in all generations, and is not weakened by time. If the Lord had mentioned an F-16 fighter jet in Scripture, it would have meant nothing to people of all previous generations. Symbolism stimulates the mind and emotions of people in any generation.

2. Symbolism interjects more emotion and feeling to the reader. This of course, separates the great novelist from the mediocre: the ability to captivate the reader. EXAMPLE: God uses "beast" to describe the world dictator we know as the Antichrist. This invokes much more emotion and awe to the reader than to call him the "one-world Dictator." It not only shows his position, but shows that he is fierce and powerful and to be feared.

3. The use of symbolism requires study and perception to grasp. The lost man, as well as the casual reader, will never unlock its truths. Remember, Jesus spoke mostly in parables to the people.

9. The Book of Revelation is a Book of Sevens.
The word seven is found thirty-one times in the book of Revelation. It is God's number of completion. The judgments during the tribulation are basically a series of sevens.
1. Seven Seals
2. Seven Trumpets
3. Seven Thunders
4. Seven Vials, or Bowls

Get a concordance and look up all the sevens in Revelation.

10. The Book of Daniel is an important book to study along with Revelation.
In most Bible college classes, Daniel and Revelation are taught together. We shall look at some of Daniel during this study. For instance, Nebuchadnezzar's vision in Daniel 2, Daniel's vision in Daniel 7, and the beast in Revelation 13 are all the same story told using different symbols.

Daniel 9:20-27 is one of the most important passages in all the Bible to grasp when studying Revelation. Turn to it and see if you can understand the "Seventy Weeks of Years," their purpose, and upon which nations of people they are determined.

This completes the introduction to the Revelation. Daniel Chapter 9 shall be the first chapter we study so we can get a firm understanding of the purpose and timeline of the Tribulation Period. Following that, a chapter by chapter study of all twenty-two chapters of Revelation. Be sure to have your Bible open, your mind alert, your heart ready, and ask the Lord to speak to you and show you great truths from His Holy Word!

DANIEL'S SEVENTIETH WEEK
Daniel 9:22-27

Daniel 9:22 "And he informed me, and talked with me, and said, O Daniel, I am now come forth to give thee skill and understanding.
23 At the beginning of thy supplications the commandment came forth, and I am come to shew thee; for thou art greatly beloved: therefore understand the matter, and consider the vision.
24 Seventy weeks are determined upon thy people and upon thy holy city, to finish the transgression, and to make an end of sins, and to make reconciliation for iniquity, and to bring in everlasting righteousness, and to seal up the vision and prophecy, and to anoint the most Holy.
25 Know therefore and understand, that from the going forth of the commandment to restore and to build Jerusalem unto the Messiah the Prince shall be seven weeks, and threescore and two weeks: the street shall be built again, and the wall, even in troublous times.
26 And after threescore and two weeks shall Messiah be cut off, but not for himself: and the people of the prince that shall come shall destroy the city and the sanctuary; and the end thereof shall be with a flood, and unto the end of the war desolations are determined.
27 And he shall confirm the covenant with many for one week: and in the midst of the week he shall cause the sacrifice and the oblation to cease, and for the overspreading of abominations he shall make it desolate, even until the consummation, and that determined shall be poured upon the desolate."

An understanding of Daniel's seventieth week in this passage will help you greatly in grasping the timeline of end time events. Let me give you a brief study of it here by just listing some points from the passage.

1. The theme of the passage is the seventy weeks.

2. These "weeks" are literally weeks of years as we see from the context.
Each week represents seven years. Seventy weeks would equal four hundred ninety years total.

3. These weeks deal with Israel, not the Church.
In verse 24 we see that "*Seventy weeks are determined upon thy people and upon thy holy city,*" and of course, the people are the Jews, and the holy city is Jerusalem. We need to get this settled right from the beginning. The Church, the people of God, are not going to be here for this seven year period called the Tribulation. It has nothing to do with the church.

4. The purpose of these seventy weeks is given in verse 24.
1. To finish the transgression
2. To make an end of sins
3. To make reconciliation
4. To bring in everlasting righteousness
5. To seal up the vision
6. To anoint the most Holy

Have you ever asked yourself why there needs to be the seven year tribulation? It is to put a final end to sin, bring reconciliation, bring to fulfillment God's prophecy, bring in righteousness, anoint the Lord Jesus Christ as King of Kings and Lord of Lord's, and begin the reign of Christ during the Millennium.

5. Sixty-nine of the seventy weeks have already been fulfilled.

In verses 24-26 of our passage, we see that this is true. Briefly, the first seven weeks (forty-nine years) took place in Ezra and Nehemiah at the building of the temple and the walls around the city. Then the next sixty-two weeks (four hundred thirty-four years) take place from Nehemiah's wall until Christ is "cut off" at Calvary. This leaves one week (seven years) yet to be fulfilled.

6. Daniel's seventieth week is yet to come.

God's time clock stopped for Israel when Christ was "cut off" and crucified at Calvary. For the last two thousand plus years we have been in the Church Age. When we come to Revelation Chapter 4, all the saved will be raptured, and God's time clock will begin again with the final week of seven years we call Daniel's seventieth week. The Church Age will be over. Look again at Daniel 9:25-26 and you will see that from the time the command came to restore and to build Jerusalem, (four hundred eighty-three years before Calvary) until it was completed, even in times of trouble and danger, was seven weeks (forty-nine years). Then another sixty-two weeks (four hundred thirty-four years) until Messiah was cut off, to pay the sin debt of the world.

Have you ever wondered why the people were waiting for the Messiah to ride into Jerusalem on what many call Palm Sunday? It is because of this timeline; they knew right to the day when Messiah was to arrive, four hundred eighty-three years after the command to build. Check Usshers dates back in Ezra and Nehemiah and add thirty-three years until Calvary and it comes out to around four hundred eighty-three years. That is why we read that many of the women in Joseph and Mary's day were hoping to be the chosen one to carry the promised Messiah, and many prophesied of His soon appearing. I am not sure they knew to the month or day He would be born, but they knew right to the day when the Messiah would enter the city. (SEE CHART ON PAGE TEN.)

7. This seventieth week (seven year tribulation) yet to come begins at the rapture in Revelation Chapter 4 and is in two, "three and one-half year periods."

Look at Daniel 9:27 and understand that in the "midst" or middle of the week of seven years, the Antichrist shall enter the temple (this temple will be built before or right after the rapture on the very spot that the Dome of the Rock occupies now), end the sacrifices, declare he is God, and break the peace treaty with Israel. Some believe that the Dome is not in the spot where the new temple will be built, but I still see it as an obstacle in the way.

Look at Matthew 24:15-24 which gives reference to what Daniel spoke of here, and calls it the "great tribulation." II Thessalonians 2:4 shows the defiling of the temple at the middle of the tribulation. Revelation 13:5-6 speaks also of this time. See below:

Matthew 24:15-24 "When ye therefore shall see the abomination of desolation, spoken of by Daniel the prophet, stand in the holy place, (whoso readeth, let him understand:) Then let them which be in Judaea flee into the mountains: Let him which is on the housetop not come down to take any thing out of his house: Neither let him which is in the field return back to take his clothes. And woe unto them that are with child, and to them that give suck in those days! But pray ye that your flight be not in the winter, neither on the sabbath day: For then shall be great tribulation, such as was not since the beginning of the world to this time, no, nor ever shall be. And except those days should be shortened, there should no flesh be saved: but for the elect's sake those days shall be shortened. Then if any man shall say unto you, Lo, here is Christ, or there; believe it not. For there shall arise false Christs, and false prophets, and shall shew great signs and wonders; insomuch that, if it were possible, they shall deceive the very elect.

2 Thessalonians 2:4 "Who opposeth and exalteth himself above all that is called God, or that is worshipped; so that he as God sitteth in the temple of God, shewing himself that he is God."

Revelation 13:5-6 "And there was given unto him a mouth speaking great things and blasphemies; and power was given unto him to continue forty and two months. And he opened his mouth in blasphemy against God, to blaspheme his name, and his tabernacle, and them that dwell in heaven."

APPLICATION:

1. The rapture is imminent; it could happen any moment.

It is the next event on God's calendar. It could happen today. Are you ready?

2. The saved will not go through the Tribulation, but instead will be raptured.

1 Thessalonians 5:9 *"For God hath not appointed us to wrath, but to obtain salvation by our Lord Jesus Christ...."*

Re 3:10 *"Because thou hast kept the word of my patience, I also will keep thee from the hour of temptation, which shall come upon all the world, to try them that dwell upon the earth."* Notice He said He would save them FROM the hour, not after the hour, or in the midst of the hour. Read again Daniel 9:24 and see that the tribulation has nothing to do with us or the church.

3. The rapture is that "blessed hope" we await.

Titus 2:13 *"Looking for that blessed hope, and the glorious appearing of the great God and our Saviour Jesus Christ...."* It would not be a blessed hope if it were at the end of the tribulation, nor would it be a hidden surprise, as we would know when the seven years were concluded.

Tribulation Time-Line Chart

Daniel's 70th Week
Daniel 9: 20-27

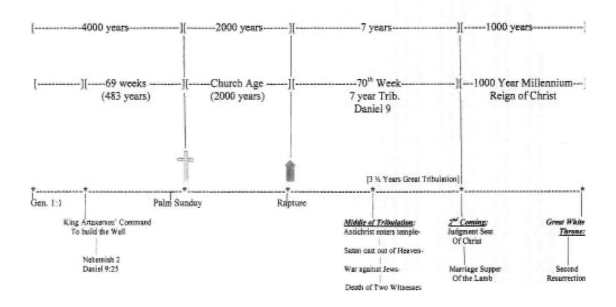

REVELATION Chapter 1

THEME: CHRIST AND HIS RELATIONSHIP TO HIS CHURCH

SUMMARY: Chapter 1 is the introduction to the book of Revelation, but also shows us the unique relationship of Christ and His church. Verse 1 lets us know it is the Revelation, or unveiling, of Jesus Christ, not John. *Revelation 1:1 "The Revelation of Jesus Christ...."*

Have you ever considered that if something must be unveiled, it must have been covered to some extent? Therefore, a person will never have the complete picture of Christ without a study of Revelation. Notice the blessing offered in verse 3 to those who read, hear, and keep the sayings of the book. Verse 4 lets us know the whole book was addressed to the seven churches existing in John's day, and we also see the Trinity in verses 4 and 5 and a reference to the precious blood of Christ. Verse 7 is a reference to the second coming AFTER the tribulation. The rapture is "*as a thief*" and occurs first, verse 7 speaks of the return of Christ after the tribulation where "*every eye shall see him.*" I like what the Bible says at the end of verse 7 concerning the terrible judgments to come: *"Even so, Amen."* In other words, "So be it." Verses 12 through 20 give the theme for the chapter:

<u>CHRIST AND HIS RELATIONSHIP TO HIS CHURCH</u> *Revelation 1:12-20 "And I turned to see the voice that spake with me. And being turned, I saw seven golden candlesticks; And in the midst of the seven candlesticks one like unto the Son of man, clothed with a garment down to the foot, and girt about the paps with a golden girdle. His head and his hairs were white like wool, as white as snow; and his eyes were as a flame of fire; And his feet like unto fine brass, as if they burned in a furnace; and his voice as the sound of many waters. And he had in his right hand seven stars: and out of his mouth went a sharp twoedged sword: and his countenance was as the sun shineth in his strength. And when I saw him, I fell at his feet as dead. And he laid his right hand upon me, saying unto me, Fear not; I am the first and the last: I am he that liveth, and was dead; and, behold, I am alive for evermore, Amen; and have the keys of hell and of death. Write the things which thou hast seen, and the things which are, and the things which shall be hereafter; The mystery of the seven stars which thou sawest in my right hand, and the seven golden candlesticks. The seven stars are the angels of the seven churches: and the seven candlesticks which thou sawest are the seven churches."*

In the above text, the symbolism is explained clearly in verse 20. Remember, the book of Revelation is full of types and symbols right from the first chapter, but take everything literally unless the context shows it is symbolic, as is the case here. Revelation is a book that uses many symbols and types to explain a very literal period we call the tribulation. (Look up <u>tribulation</u> in a concordance)

The candlesticks represent churches and the stars are the angels, the pastors of the churches. There is no doubt that these are no heavenly angels when you consider that John was to write letters to these angels, or is this the first instance of AIR MAIL? No, angels have often brought a message to man, but never the other way around. We see that Christ has these pastors in his right hand signifying ownership, control, and honor. The fact that seven churches are mentioned can either mean there were seven local churches in existence at that time, or may simply refer to God's number of completeness, and the seven could represent all churches. Verse 12 says these churches were all in Asia, so I lean towards the latter. Precious gold is used to refer to His church, signifying its value. Verses 13-15 show a symbolic description of Jesus, the head of the church! Wisdom, power, discernment, and judgment are seen in these verses.

LESSONS:

1. The church belongs to Christ.
   a) He started the church. Matthew 16:18 *"And I say also unto thee, That thou art Peter, and upon this rock I will build my church; and the gates of hell shall not prevail against it."*
   b) He purchased it with His own blood. Acts 20:28 *"Take heed therefore unto yourselves, and to all the flock, over the which the Holy Ghost hath made you overseers, to feed the church of God, which he hath purchased with his own blood."*

2. The church is precious to Christ. Notice He calls it a "golden candlestick" in Revelation 1:12.

3. He loves the church dearly. Ephesians 5:25 *"Husbands, love your wives, even as Christ also loved the church, and gave himself for it...."*

4. He, as owner, chastens and purges His church. Ephesians 5:25-27 *"Husbands, love your wives, even as Christ also loved the church, and gave himself for it; That he might sanctify and cleanse it with the washing of water by the word, That he might present it to himself a glorious church, not having spot, or wrinkle, or any such thing; but that it should be holy and without blemish."*
   The church will be the bride of Christ after the rapture. We are espoused to Him now, but we will not be the bride until the rapture. Christ, as owner, sets the rules and guidelines for the church, not man. (Do our church by-laws fit the Bible?)

5. Christ has set pastors over His churches to lead them. The seven stars in Revelation 1:16,20 are the pastors. We see them again in Revelation Chapters 2 and 3.
   See also: Ephesians 4:11-12: *"And he gave some, apostles; and some, prophets; and some, evangelists; and some, pastors and teachers; For the perfecting of the saints, for the work of the ministry, for the edifying of the body of Christ:"*
   In Acts 20:28, which is addressed to the Pastors, the Overseers, He says: *"Take heed therefore unto yourselves, and to all the flock, over the which the Holy Ghost hath made you overseers, to feed the church of God, which he hath purchased with his own blood."*
   See also: Hebrews 13:7 *"Remember them which have the rule over you, who have spoken unto you the word of God: whose faith follow, considering the end of their conversation."*
   Hebrews 13:17 *"Obey them that have the rule over you, and submit yourselves: for they watch for your souls, as they that must give account, that they may do it with joy, and not with grief: for that is unprofitable for you."*
   1 Peter 5:3 *"Neither as being lords over God's heritage, but being ensamples to the flock."*

PERSONAL APPLICATION:

I. Everyone should be an active member of the local church. Acts 2:41-47
   You do not have to join a church to be saved, but my friend, it is a dangerous thing to be outside of the church that Jesus established and purchased with His own blood. I do not believe in the big, spooky, invisible, universal church, but regardless of what you

believe, I challenge you to find where God dealt with or did anything without going through the LOCAL CHURCH. Let me give a few examples:

1. Cornelius in Acts 10 was led to Christ by Peter, a member of the local church. God did not bypass the church, but rather sent an angel to give instruction to Cornelius to send for Peter. The great commission of Matthew 28:19-20 is given to the church, not individuals. Part of that commission is baptizing them, or did you think you have the authority to baptize your converts in the bathtub at home? No, of course not. It is a church ordinance, and our soul winning should be done under the canopy and authority of the church as well.

2. In Acts 13:1-4 Paul was sent out from his church to go start churches.

In fact, in this passage it seems the church leadership knew the Lord's will before Paul did. *"Now there were in the church that was at Antioch certain prophets and teachers; as Barnabas, and Simeon that was called Niger, and Lucius of Cyrene, and Manaen, which had been brought up with Herod the tetrarch, and Saul. As they ministered to the Lord, and fasted, the Holy Ghost said, Separate me Barnabas and Saul for the work whereunto I have called them. And when they had fasted and prayed, and laid their hands on them, they sent them away. So they, being sent forth by the Holy Ghost, departed unto Seleucia; and from thence they sailed to Cyprus."*

3. The New Testament was written directly and at times indirectly to the church, not individuals. I realize some books were addressed to an individual, but God used them indirectly as Scripture for the church. The Bible speaks best to those within His local church.

II. Everyone should develop a love for the church.

If Christ loves it, and it is important to Him, we should love it too. Try thinking about and praying for your fellow members and see if you do not fall in love with them. The reason so many do not develop a love for their church is they do not spend enough time with the people of their church. You can not really love Christ without loving and being a faithful part of the church He loves and shed His blood for.

III. Everyone should be faithful to church.

Every time the doors are open, I should be in my place, and get involved as much as I can. Thomas is known to us as "Doubting Thomas" because he missed church one time.

See John 21:24-25, *"This is the disciple which testifieth of these things, and wrote these things: and we know that his testimony is true. And there are also many other things which Jesus did, the which, if they should be written every one, I suppose that even the world itself could not contain the books that should be written. Amen."*

Our faith is increased as we here the preaching and teaching of the Word of God. Romans 10:17 *"So then faith cometh by hearing, and hearing by the word of God."*

IV. The church you attend should be like a family to you.

The Bible says we are God's children when we get saved. That means we are brothers and sisters in Christ. John 1:12, *"But as many as received him, to them gave he power to become the sons of God, even to them that believe on his name:"*

Please do not misunderstand what I am going to say next, but I believe you should be closer to your church family than you are to your earthly family. Of course, blessed is the person who gets his earthly family saved! Do you realize that we are going to spend eternity with our "family in Christ," and not necessarily with our "earthly family?" The truth is, Christ drives a wedge between saved and lost family members.

See Matthew 10:34-36, *"Think not that I am come to send peace on earth: I came not to send peace, but a sword. For I am come to set a man at variance against his father, and the daughter against her mother, and the daughter in law against her mother in law. And a man's foes shall be they of his own household."*

CLOSING: Wow, what a church! What an honor and responsibility that is ours! We are part of an institution started and headed up by Christ himself! This is a church that is promised divine perpetuity, a church that shall never end. Kingdoms come, institutions come, men rise to power, but they all come to an end. Glory to God, the church will NEVER end, and we can be a part of it. We will soon be assembled in heaven as the bride of Christ!

REVELATION Chapters 2 and 3

THEME: LETTERS TO THE SEVEN CHURCHES - THE CHURCH AGE

SUMMARY:

In Chapter 1, we saw Christ and His relationship to the church, His church. In Chapters 2 and 3 we will see letters that John was told to write and send to these seven churches in Asia. They are mentioned by name in Revelation 1:11 *"Saying, I am Alpha and Omega, the first and the last: and, What thou seest, write in a book, and send it unto the seven churches which are in Asia; unto Ephesus, and unto Smyrna, and unto Pergamos, and unto Thyatira, and unto Sardis, and unto Philadelphia, and unto Laodicea."* John is told to write these letters and address them to the pastors of these churches. Revelation 2:1 *"Unto the angel of the church of Ephesus write;"* and the same is said of the following six churches. The angel is the pastor, the star in the right hand of Jesus, and is responsible for the direction and stand of the church. Revelation 1:20 *"The mystery of the seven stars which thou sawest in my right hand, and the seven golden candlesticks. The seven stars are the angels of the seven churches: and the seven candlesticks which thou sawest are the seven churches."*

These are actual literal churches that existed in 96 A.D. We will see the different characteristics of each of these churches, but there is a deeper, more prophetic meaning concerning these seven churches. Revelation is a prophetic book, is it not? These seven churches were chosen by Christ because each had the characteristics that would dominate each of the seven ages of church history, from Jesus to the rapture.

Go through Chapters 2 and 3 in your Bible and highlight the names of each of the seven churches so you can find them easily. Let me list and explain some of the things said to each church. For the sake of being brief, I will not mention everything, but will just point out a few things about each church. As we go through this, remember that these are actual churches of John's day that had these actual characteristics mentioned, but at the same time represent the two thousand plus years of the church age, and the condition of the church as a whole throughout each age. This church age was future for John, it is mostly past for us, as we are now living in the last age, the Laodicean age. As I briefly describe the characteristics of each of the seven churches below, keep in mind that these are the characteristics of these literal churches that John was writing to, as well as the general condition of the churchs throughout the church age.

The church in Ephesus:

Revelation 2:1-7 *"Unto the angel of the church of Ephesus write; These things saith he that holdeth the seven stars in his right hand, who walketh in the midst of the seven golden candlesticks; I know thy works, and thy labour, and thy patience, and how thou canst not bear them which are evil: and thou hast tried them which say they are apostles, and are not, and hast found them liars: And hast borne, and hast patience, and for my name's sake hast laboured, and hast not fainted. Nevertheless I have somewhat against thee, because thou hast left thy first love. Remember therefore from whence thou art fallen, and repent, and do the first works; or else I will come unto thee quickly, and will remove thy candlestick out of his place, except thou repent. But this thou hast, that thou hatest the deeds of the Nicolaitans, which I also hate. He that hath an ear, let him hear what the Spirit saith unto the churches; To him that overcometh will I give to eat of the tree of life, which is in the midst of the paradise of God."*

The church in Ephesus was a good church, a hard working church, yet it had left its first love. This may mean they had left their love for the Lord and were working hard, not out of love, but rather duty. They had a hatred for sin, they worked hard, but had left their love for Christ. It could also mean they no longer had a concern for sinners, and had quit seeking the lost, as this is certainly the great heartbeat of God and the great commission of the church. They hated sin, and perhaps had quit winning souls to fight sin. Likewise many churches today have quit reaching souls to fight the battle against abortion or homosexuality, or to get involved in politics.

Ephesus means "desirable one." This church is prophetic of the first century of the Church Age. This church is a working church, a sin-hating church, but had gotten its priorities wrong. As this happened in the first century, so it happens today.

The church in Smyrna:
Revelation 2:8-11, "*And unto the angel of the church in Smyrna write; These things saith the first and the last, which was dead, and is alive;*
9 I know thy works, and tribulation, and poverty, (but thou art rich) and I know the blasphemy of them which say they are Jews, and are not, but are the synagogue of Satan.
10 Fear none of those things which thou shalt suffer: behold, the devil shall cast some of you into prison, that ye may be tried; and ye shall have <u>*tribulation ten days:*</u> *be thou faithful unto death, and I will give thee a crown of life.*
11 He that hath an ear, let him hear what the Spirit saith unto the churches; He that overcometh shall not be hurt of the second death."

The church in Smyrna was a poor and suffering church. It was under persecution, and some members were even imprisoned. The name *Smyrna*, comes from the word *myrrh*, a spice used as a perfume by Israel. This spice gave off a fragrance, but only after it was crushed and beaten did it give off its full fragrance. It is one of the gifts the wise men brought to Jesus, and pictures the suffering he would endure to bring about a sweet sacrificial offering to the Father for our sin. Smyrna means "suffering," and is a fitting description of this church that was persecuted and suffered tribulation. This church is prophetic of the Church Age of the years from 100-313 A.D. If you study history, you will find that this was a time of great persecution of Christians. Notice I underlined ten days of tribulation above. I believe this is a reference to the ten Roman emperors that ruled during this time, from Nero to Constantine. Just as myrrh, the people of God were crushed and beaten under these ten Roman persecutions.

The church was admonished to be "*faithful unto death.*" Nothing negative is said about this church. Surely there was something the Lord could have said, but I am reminded of the verse in Matthew 12:20, "*A bruised reed shall he not break, and smoking flax shall he not quench, until he send forth judgment unto victory.*" The Lord will not lay on us more than we can handle.

The church in Pergamos:
Revelation 2:12 "*And to the angel of the church in Pergamos write; These things saith he which hath the sharp sword with two edges;*
13 I know thy works, and where thou dwellest, even where Satan's seat is: and thou holdest fast my name, and hast not denied my faith, even in those days wherein Antipas was my faithful martyr, who was slain among you, where Satan dwelleth.
14 But I have a few things against thee, because thou hast there them that hold the doctrine of Balaam,

who taught Balac to cast a stumblingblock before the children of Israel, to eat things sacrificed unto idols, and to commit fornication.

15 So hast thou also them that hold the doctrine of the Nicolaitans, which thing I hate.

16 Repent; or else I will come unto thee quickly, and will fight against them with the sword of my mouth.

17 He that hath an ear, let him hear what the Spirit saith unto the churches; To him that overcometh will I give to eat of the hidden manna, and will give him a white stone, and in the stone a new name written, which no man knoweth saving he that receiveth it."

The church in Pergamos appears to be a church located in a place that is a stronghold for Satan. Pergamos means "marriage," and this church was married to the world. In other words, they were not separated, and had yoked up with the world. If you were to have visited this church, you would have had a hard time seeing any difference between the church and the world. You could say they were a worldly church. This church is prophetic of the third Church Age between 313-590 A.D.

This fits the time of the supposed conversion of Constantine, when he is said to have seen a sign in the heavens. Constantine merged, or married together, the church and the state. The roots of Roman Catholicism go back to him. When Constantine died, he was placed in the center of twelve coffins, as if to say he was greater than the twelve Apostles.

Though this church is praised for their stand, the Lord mentions two doctrines that were allowed to be taught and practiced of which they were told to repent.

1. Doctrine of Balaam: Lack of separation, which brings worldliness. See Numbers 22:5 and II Peter 2:15.

2. Doctrine of the Nicolaitans: Basically, the false belief that the laity needs a clergyman to communicate for him to God. The word literally means to conquer the laity. The Catholic as well as some Protestant churches seem to fit this mold. God hates this doctrine!

The church in Thyatira:

Revelation 2:18 "And unto the angel of the church in Thyatira write; These things saith the Son of God, who hath his eyes like unto a flame of fire, and his feet are like fine brass;

19 I know thy works, and charity, and service, and faith, and thy patience, and thy works; and the last to be more than the first.

20 Notwithstanding I have a few things against thee, because thou sufferest that woman Jezebel, which calleth herself a prophetess, to teach and to seduce my servants to commit fornication, and to eat things sacrificed unto idols.

21 And I gave her space to repent of her fornication; and she repented not.

22 Behold, I will cast her into a bed, and them that commit adultery with her into great tribulation, except they repent of their deeds.

23 And I will kill her children with death; and all the churches shall know that I am he which searcheth the reins and hearts: and I will give unto every one of you according to your works.

24 But unto you I say, and unto the rest in Thyatira, as many as have not this doctrine, and which have not known the depths of Satan, as they speak; I will put upon you none other burden.

25 But that which ye have already hold fast until I come.

26 And he that overcometh, and keepeth my works unto the end, to him will I give power over the nations:

27 And he shall rule them with a rod of iron; as the vessels of a potter shall they be broken to shivers: even as I received of my Father.

28 And I will give him the morning star.

29 He that hath an ear, let him hear what the Spirit saith unto the churches."

The church in Thyatira is bragged upon for their good works, charity, faith, and patience. Then the Lord rebukes them for allowing the teaching of Jezebel into the church. Now I do not think this is speaking literally of a woman, as I think the context shows, but rather it is speaking figuratively. I believe this church had allowed the wicked teachings of false religion to enter in. Jezebel is used as a type of this wicked teaching of sacrifices, ceremonies, rites, rituals and the adding of works to the gospel of grace.

Thyatira means "continual sacrifice" and is prophetic of the fourth Church Age from 590-1500. This, of course, is the rise of Roman Catholicism which really got its start under Constantine. When a church does not practice separation from the world and false religion, it becomes watered down. The continual sacrifice is none other than the mass, coupled with doing penance or other works to maintain your salvation. This age is also known as the dark ages. Remember, this is an actual church that existed in John's day. The church was not separated and had allowed a works salvation to creep into its doctrine, but it also is prophetic of a one thousand year age of the church known as the dark ages.

The church in Sardis:

Revelation 3:1 "And unto the angel of the church in Sardis write; These things saith he that hath the seven Spirits of God, and the seven stars; I know thy works, that thou hast a name that thou livest, and art dead.
2 Be watchful, and strengthen the things which remain, that are ready to die: for I have not found thy works perfect before God.
3 Remember therefore how thou hast received and heard, and hold fast, and repent. If therefore thou shalt not watch, I will come on thee as a thief, and thou shalt not know what hour I will come upon thee.
4 Thou hast a few names even in Sardis which have not defiled their garments; and they shall walk with me in white: for they are worthy.
5 He that overcometh, the same shall be clothed in white raiment; and I will not blot out his name out of the book of life, but I will confess his name before my Father, and before his angels.
6 He that hath an ear, let him hear what the Spirit saith unto the churches."

The church in Sardis is spoken of in a negative light first, which is unlike the other four we have seen. They are said in verse 1 to have a name that they do not live up to. This reminds me of many saved folks today that are called Christian, but do not live up to that name. The Lord says in verse 4 that there are a few that are living for him. Praise the Lord for the few! Sardis means "a remnant," and is prophetic of the Church Age from 1500-1700.

This is the time in history that we had the first printing press invented by Johann Gutenburg in 1550. The Bible was the first book printed. It was during this time that the Bible became accessible to the common man. What a difference this made in history! Now people could have their eyes opened to the great truths from Scripture. Martin Luther would begin the Reformation, along with other great men like Erasmus, Calvin, Zwingli, and others. While I do not agree with all the doctrine of these men, they were greatly used of God.

The church in Philadelphia:

Revelation 3:7 "And to the angel of the church in Philadelphia write; These things saith he that is holy, he that is true, he that hath the key of David, he that openeth, and no man shutteth; and shutteth, and no man openeth;

8 I know thy works: behold, I have set before thee an open door, and no man can shut it: for thou hast a little strength, and hast kept my word, and hast not denied my name.

9 Behold, I will make them of the synagogue of Satan, which say they are Jews, and are not, but do lie; behold, I will make them to come and worship before thy feet, and to know that I have loved thee.

10 Because thou hast kept the word of my patience, I also will keep thee from the hour of temptation, which shall come upon all the world, to try them that dwell upon the earth.

11 Behold, I come quickly: hold that fast which thou hast, that no man take thy crown.

12 Him that overcometh will I make a pillar in the temple of my God, and he shall go no more out: and I will write upon him the name of my God, and the name of the city of my God, which is new Jerusalem, which cometh down out of heaven from my God: and I will write upon him my new name.

13 He that hath an ear, let him hear what the Spirit saith unto the churches."

This was the church with the open door, a soul winning church. There was nothing negative said about this church, which shows the great heart of God for reaching the lost. No man can shut a door that God has opened, nor can one open a door that God has shut. We see this in Noah's day when God shut the door of the Ark.

Philadelphia means "brotherly love" and is prophetic of the sixth church age from 1700-1901. It was the age of the great awakenings and many revivals. This was the age of great leaders like George Whitefield, the boy preacher with the golden voice, that could be heard a mile away with no microphone. Men like Jonathan Edwards and his famous sermon, "Sinners in the hands of an angry God" in which he likens man to a spider hanging over a fire by just a web. It was said that grown men were crying out for mercy and grabbing the pillars in the church to keep from falling into hell! It was the age of men like John Wesley, Spurgeon, Moody, and many others. It was the age of open doors, of revival and the great moving of God. It was a time when men not only had Bibles, but also had great faith in God's Word as we see in Revelation 3:8 *"..and hast kept my word...."* The Lord promises that they will not go through the tribulation in Revelation 3:10. Now this is important, not only does it back up the many other scriptures that teach a pre-tribulation rapture, but also shows that there will be Philadelphia churches in existence right through the Laodicean Age and up to the rapture.

The church in Laodicea:

Revelation 3:14 "And unto the angel of the church of the Laodiceans write; These things saith the Amen, the faithful and true witness, the beginning of the creation of God;

15 I know thy works, that thou art neither cold nor hot: I would thou wert cold or hot.

16 So then because thou art lukewarm, and neither cold nor hot, I will spue thee out of my mouth.

17 Because thou sayest, I am rich, and increased with goods, and have need of nothing; and knowest not that thou art wretched, and miserable, and poor, and blind, and naked:

18 I counsel thee to buy of me gold tried in the fire, that thou mayest be rich; and white raiment, that thou mayest be clothed, and that the shame of thy nakedness do not appear; and anoint thine eyes with eyesalve, that thou mayest see.

19 As many as I love, I rebuke and chasten: be zealous therefore, and repent.

20 Behold, I stand at the door, and knock: if any man hear my voice, and open the door, I will come in to him, and will sup with him, and he with me.

21 To him that overcometh will I grant to sit with me in my throne, even as I also overcame, and am set down with my Father in his throne.

22 He that hath an ear, let him hear what the Spirit saith unto the churches."

The church of Laodicea has nothing good said about it. They were lukewarm. They feel rich, yet the Lord says they are poor, blind, miserable, and wretched! It was the time in which everyone wants their rights. Just think about that for a minute in light of the time we live in. Everyone wants their rights, from women's rights, to animal rights, to gay rights. Children want their rights, unions want their rights, minorities, prisoners, and on and on we could go. I have a sermon I call "God has rights too" but in this age, people are not concerned with God's rights.

In verse 20 we see the Lord actually standing outside the church knocking, wanting to be let in. How sad that many churches today have actually put Christ out of their church.

Laodicea means "the rights of the people," and is prophetic of the final age of the church from 1901 until the rapture in Revelation Chapter 4. It is the age we are living in right now, and is the worst of the seven church ages. The one that makes God want to VOMIT! Never in history have a people that have so much done so little for God!

This chart will help you see and comprehend these seven ages of the church. It will be helpful if you study the chart and review what you have learned. At the bottom of the chart is another brief summary of the Church Age.

CHART OF THE SEVEN AGES OF CHURCH HISTORY

1. Ephesus ----- means desirable one...First Century
2. Smyrna ----- comes from the word myrrh, signifying suffering........................100-300
3. Pergamos ----- means marriage, as in married to the state or world...............300-500
4. Thyatira ----- means continual sacrifice, (works, mass, ceremonies, dark ages, etc.) 500-1500
5. Sardis ----- means remnant (we see this during the reformation period) 1500-1700
6. Philadelphia ----- means brotherly love.... Great awakenings, revivals, Edwards, Whitfield -----1700-1901
7. Laodicean ----- means the rights of the people ...just look around today! ---1901-rapture

* Dates are approximate

BRIEF SUMMARY OF THE SEVEN AGES OF THE CHURCH

The church in Ephesus represents the first one hundred years of history, also called the Apostolic Age. This is during the days of the Apostles, including Paul's missionary journeys.

The church in Smyrna represents the next two hundred years from 100-313 A.D. when Constantine showed up. It is said that Polycarp, a convert of John, was the pastor in Smyrna. History gives us record of ten Roman emperors who persecuted the church during this time. Compare that to Revelation 2:10 *"Fear none of those things which thou shalt suffer: behold, the devil shall cast some of you into prison, that ye may be tried; and ye shall have tribulation ten days...."* Nero was the first of those ten wicked emperors who brought terrible persecution to the church. In A.D. 156 Polycarp was given the choice to revile Christ or be burned at the stake to which he made this famous reply: "Eighty and six years have I served him and He never did me any harm; how then can I blaspheme my King and my Saviour?"

The church in Pergamos represents the age from 313-590 A.D. Pergamos is defined "marriage." The Church united with the state, or the world if you will. The church became the state religion, and the political leader, Constantine, became the religious leader. Much of Catholic doctrine stems from this age, including the practice of the doctrines of Balaam and the Nicolaitans.

The church in Thyatira represents the age from 590-1500's also known as "The Dark Ages." The name Thyatira means "continual sacrifice." It symbolizes the works, ceremonies, and rituals such as "the mass", Mary worship and good deeds that were added to the gospel.

The church in Sardis represents the Reformation Age from 1500-1700 during the times of Luther, Calvin, and others. The printing press was invented in 1550 with a Bible being the first complete book ever printed! The Bible in the hands of the common man soon opened many of the people's eyes to the truth. Be very careful about following someone who thinks that the Bible is a book for the "clergy" and not the common man. 2 Peter 1:20-21 *Knowing this first, that no prophecy of the scripture is of any private interpretation. For the prophecy came not in old time by the will of man: but holy men of God spake as they were moved by the Holy Ghost.*

The church in Philadelphia covers 1700's-1901 and is the time of great revivals and the two great awakenings. Philadelphia means "brotherly love." God raised up some great men like George Whitfield, and Jonathan Edwards who preached the famous sermon "Sinners in the Hand's of an Angry God." Men like Spurgeon and Moody shook whole continents for God in the 1800's! America arose as the Christian nation of the world, and to this day still sends out more fundamental Christian missionaries than any other nation.

The church in Laodicea covers 1901 until the rapture. This age is by far the worst of them all. Why 1901 you might ask? It is the very year that the RSV translation of the Bible came to America. For the first time in our great American history, we now had two authorities, two Bibles. It has been downhill from there ever since. I heard recently, that the NIV is now out- selling the King James Bible. What a shame, but just look at Revelation 3:14-20 and see if it is not describing our churches today. There has not been much revival to speak of since 1901. Our churches are cold, our people are pleasure seekers, proud, unfaithful, covetous, and have very little convictions. Our churches are rocked by sin and immorality, people are easily offended, preachers are either running off with the secretary or refusing to preach against sin. The charismatic movement has infiltrated our people with false doctrine and emotionalism that will one day lead to a worship of the Antichrist! We had better get ready, the trumpet is preparing to sound, the rapture could occur at any moment, all things are now ready.

How about you, are you ready to meet the Lord?

LESSONS:

I: The seven churches have three interpretations:

1. These are seven literal churches that existed at that day. They give us insight into Christ's ownership of and relationship to the church. They also shows us the relationship between the pastor and the Lord. These churches show us what a church should be, as well as some things a church should not be. This would be the literal interpretation. Always take the Bible literally unless the context shows otherwise. Remember though, even literal passages have spiritual truths and spiritual application for us today.

2. Truths concerning these seven churches can also be applied to the Christian life. For instance, the church in Ephesus had left its first love. You and I should examine our own lives. Do we have the love for Christ and a love for souls that we once had? Take some time to consider the good and bad about each church and see how you measure up.

3. Prophetic meaning to show the entire age of the church

Though I believe that these are literal churches that existed in John's day, **I believe the main prophetic teaching concerning these churches is that they represent the seven ages of church history.** Let me give you some reasons why I am certain of this:

A) Because the first verse of Revelation shows that it is a prophetic book of things to come. See Revelation 1:1 "*The Revelation of Jesus Christ, which God gave unto him, to shew unto his servants things which must <u>shortly come to pass;</u> and he sent and signified it by his angel unto his servant John:*"

B) Because of its chronological order in the book. The rapture takes place in Chapter 4 right after the last of the seven churches is mentioned, and that last church is a cold and dead church that the Bible says will exist at the time of the rapture.

C) Because the very names of the seven churches fit the timeline perfectly as well as the description given about the churches.

D) Because looking back, we can clearly see all seven of these church ages in history.

II: Attributes of the Lord in each passage

Remember, the Revelation is the unveiling of Jesus Christ! Each of the letters to the seven churches give us some attributes of Him. I have listed a few of them here.

Revelation 2:1 "These things saith he that holdeth the seven stars in his right hand, who walketh in the midst of the seven golden candlesticks...." His presence and Lordship.

Revelation 2:8 "These things saith the first and the last, which was dead, and is alive...." Praise the Lord, he always was, and always will be! He is alive and well!

Revelation 2:12 "These things saith he which hath the sharp sword with two edges...." Sword of judgment.

Revelation 2:18 "These things saith the Son of God, who hath his eyes like unto a flame of fire, and his feet are like fine brass...." Discernment and judgment.

Revelation 3:1 "These things saith he that hath the seven Spirits of God, and the seven stars...." Omniscience.

Revelation 3:7 "These things saith he that is holy, he that is true, he that hath the key of David, he that openeth, and no man shutteth; and shutteth, and no man openeth...." Holy and true, all powerful.

Revelation 3:14 "These things saith the Amen, the faithful and true witness, the beginning of the creation of God...."

III: A church can lose its charter

Jesus commands "*repent, and do the first works; or else I will come unto thee quickly, and will remove thy candlestick out of his place, except thou repent.*" (Revelation 2:5) We see a similar warning in Revelation 2:16 as well. What this means is that if a church will not repent in an area, Jesus will remove His candlestick, His franchise, or charter. It may still have a building, pews, and Sunday services, but it is no longer a New Testament church. The candlestick has been removed. I believe there are many churches in America that have services each week, but in fact are no longer New Testament churches.

PERSONAL APPLICATION:

1. Be sure you are a part of a good local church that is pleasing to God.
2. Ask yourself, "Which of these seven churches would best compare to the church that I attend?"
3. The pastor is God's representative, the "angel" of the church; be sure you show him respect and honor.
4. To not understand the sober reality of the Laodicean Age we live in will lead to frustration and depression for the servant of God.
5. Even though there do not seem to be any great revivals mentioned during the last age, that is not to say that your home church or you yourself can not experience revival. Do not fall for this false teaching that says we cannot win souls or do much for God during this age. God has not changed, and God's promises have not changed.

CLOSING:

We are right now in the Laodicean Age, which is last of the Church Age. The coming of Christ is near, the trumpet could sound at any moment and Christ will take all believers off this earth in what we call the Rapture. In Revelation Chapter 4, we shall see what takes place in heaven at the rapture. My friend, are you ready to meet the Lord? Are you ready to see Him face to face?

REVELATION Chapter 4

THEME: THE RAPTURE

SUMMARY:

Revelation 4:1-11 "After this I looked, and, behold, a door was opened in heaven: and the first voice which I heard was as it were of a trumpet talking with me; which said, Come up hither, and I will shew thee things which must be hereafter. And immediately I was in the spirit: and, behold, a throne was set in heaven, and one sat on the throne. And he that sat was to look upon like a jasper and a sardine stone: and there was a rainbow round about the throne, in sight like unto an emerald. And round about the throne were four and twenty seats: and upon the seats I saw four and twenty elders sitting, clothed in white raiment; and they had on their heads crowns of gold. And out of the throne proceeded lightnings and thunderings and voices: and there were seven lamps of fire burning before the throne, which are the seven Spirits of God. And before the throne there was a sea of glass like unto crystal: and in the midst of the throne, and round about the throne, were four beasts full of eyes before and behind. And the first beast was like a lion, and the second beast like a calf, and the third beast had a face as a man, and the fourth beast was like a flying eagle. And the four beasts had each of them six wings about him; and they were full of eyes within: and they rest not day and night, saying, Holy, holy, holy, Lord God Almighty, which was, and is, and is to come. And when those beasts give glory and honour and thanks to him that sat on the throne, who liveth for ever and ever, The four and twenty elders fall down before him that sat on the throne, and worship him that liveth for ever and ever, and cast their crowns before the throne, saying, Thou art worthy, O Lord, to receive glory and honour and power: for thou hast created all things, and for thy pleasure they are and were created."

In Chapter 1, we saw Christ in the midst of the seven golden candlesticks. In Chapters 2 and 3 we saw the seven letters written to the seven churches, and we clearly saw that these seven churches have a prophetic meaning. We saw that they represented seven ages of church history. When we begin Chapter 4, we see something has changed. The view has now changed from earth to heaven.

Look at Revelation 4:1: *"After this I looked, and, behold, a door was opened in heaven: and the first voice which I heard was as it were of a trumpet talking with me; which said, Come up hither, and I will shew thee things which must be hereafter."*

This is the rapture, the calling away of all believers. Compare the voice as a trumpet, with I Thessalonians 4:16-17 *"For the Lord himself shall descend from heaven with a shout, with the voice of the archangel, and with the trump of God: and the dead in Christ shall rise first: Then we which are alive and remain shall be caught up together with them in the clouds, to meet the Lord in the air: and so shall we ever be with the Lord."*

See and compare also I Corinthians 15:52 *"In a moment, in the twinkling of an eye, at the last trump: for the trumpet shall sound, and the dead shall be raised incorruptible, and we shall be changed."*

This is an amazing chapter to read! Just imagine, John is caught up into heaven, he is about to see and experience exactly what all of us who are saved and alive at the rapture will partake of. Look at the passage. In verse 2 we see that the very first thing we shall behold at the rapture is the throne, and He that sits on that throne. When we get to Chapter 5, we shall see without any doubt that it is God the Father, not Jesus on the throne.

Next, in verse 4, we see the twenty-four elders sitting on seats and having crowns on their heads. It is my opinion that these twenty-four elders are the twelve Old Testament Patriarchs and the twelve Apostles from the New Testament. I believe they represent

24

all the saved in heaven. The "white raiment" is clothing of the redeemed, and there are no redeemed angels, so these must be saved men. Verse 5 seems to be referring to the Holy Spirit, the third Person of the Trinity. The four beasts in verse 6 are living creatures created to praise God night and day. In verses 10-11 we see that the twenty-four elders fall down and worship the Lord, and cast their crowns at His feet. Perhaps the crowns are another clue as to the identity of the elders. They seem to be a type of all the redeemed at the rapture. The four beasts in verses 6-8 are created beings that give praise to God. You can read more about them in Ezekiel Chapter 5. The end of verse 11 tells us that we were made for the pleasure of God.

Chapter 4 is the rapture, the end of the church age, and the beginning of Daniel's seventieth week, the Tribulation which lasts seven years.

LESSONS:
1. The word <u>rapture</u> is not in the Bible, but is derived from "caught up" in
I Thessalonians 4:16
2. The rapture is the next event on God's time clock. There are no prophecies that must be fulfilled before the rapture can occur. His coming is imminent. He could come today.
3. This will be the rapture of all believers, not the church.

Nowhere in the Bible is there any reference to the church being called out. It is the calling out of all the saved people. It is true that saved people make up the church, but not all the saved are part of the local church. All believers will not make up the church, the spotless bride of Christ, until the rapture. The doctrine of the universal, spooky, invisible church is not taught in the Bible.
4. The rapture is the "blessed hope" of Titus 2:13 because it removes us from the terrible time to come upon the world known as the tribulation.
5. We were created for the praise and glory of God. (Revelation 4:11)

We have no right to do our own thing, we have no right to live for self. God made us with a purpose: to bring glory to Him.

PERSONAL APPLICATION:
1. Ask yourself, am I 100% sure I am saved and ready to meet the Lord at the rapture?
2. Will I have a crown to cast at His feet?

1 Corinthians 3:11-15 "For other foundation can no man lay than that is laid, which is Jesus Christ. Now if any man build upon this foundation gold, silver, precious stones, wood, hay, stubble; Every man's work shall be made manifest: for the day shall declare it, because it shall be revealed by fire; and the fire shall try every man's work of what sort it is. If any man's work abide which he hath built thereupon, he shall receive a reward. If any man's work shall be burned, he shall suffer loss: but he himself shall be saved; yet so as by fire."

Some will have a crown, and some will be left standing in the ashes. Many people are "saved yet so as by fire" and will have no reward in heaven.
3. Am I bringing pleasure to God? Is my life pleasing to him? Would I be ashamed if He came tonight?

CLOSING:

The rapture is the next event on God's calendar. Do not miss it by not getting saved. If you have heard the gospel but have put off getting saved, you will not get a second chance after the rapture. See II Thessalonians 2:1-12 and note especially verses 9-12.

REVELATION Chapter 5

THEME: THE SEVEN SEALED BOOK - TITLE DEED TO THE EARTH

SUMMARY:

Revelation 5:1-14 "And I saw in the right hand of him that sat on the throne a book written within and on the backside, sealed with seven seals. And I saw a strong angel proclaiming with a loud voice, Who is worthy to open the book, and to loose the seals thereof? And no man in heaven, nor in earth, neither under the earth, was able to open the book, neither to look thereon. And I wept much, because no man was found worthy to open and to read the book, neither to look thereon. And one of the elders saith unto me, Weep not: behold, the Lion of the tribe of Juda, the Root of David, hath prevailed to open the book, and to loose the seven seals thereof. And I beheld, and, lo, in the midst of the throne and of the four beasts, and in the midst of the elders, stood a Lamb as it had been slain, having seven horns and seven eyes, which are the seven Spirits of God sent forth into all the earth. And he came and took the book out of the right hand of him that sat upon the throne. And when he had taken the book, the four beasts and four and twenty elders fell down before the Lamb, having every one of them harps, and golden vials full of odours, which are the prayers of saints. And they sung a new song, saying, Thou art worthy to take the book, and to open the seals thereof: for thou wast slain, and hast redeemed us to God by thy blood out of every kindred, and tongue, and people, and nation; And hast made us unto our God kings and priests: and we shall reign on the earth. And I beheld, and I heard the voice of many angels round about the throne and the beasts and the elders: and the number of them was ten thousand times ten thousand, and thousands of thousands; Saying with a loud voice, Worthy is the Lamb that was slain to receive power, and riches, and wisdom, and strength, and honour, and glory, and blessing. And every creature which is in heaven, and on the earth, and under the earth, and such as are in the sea, and all that are in them, heard I saying, Blessing, and honour, and glory, and power, be unto him that sitteth upon the throne, and unto the Lamb for ever and ever. And the four beasts said, Amen. And the four and twenty elders fell down and worshipped him that liveth for ever and ever."

In Chapter 1, we saw Christ in the midst of the seven golden candlesticks. In Chapters 2 and 3 we saw the seven letters written to the seven churches, and we clearly saw that these seven churches have a prophetic meaning. We see that they represent the entire Church Age. We are living in the final hours of the last Church Age right now! (Study the signs of the times given in II Timothy 3.) When we began Chapter 4, the trump of God had sounded and all believers were taken to heaven. Chapter 5 verse 1 begins with a glimpse of One sitting on the throne, and a book in His right hand. The One on the throne is the Father, the book is the title deed to the earth. The devil is the god of this world right now, and part of the purpose of the tribulation is to redeem the earth from the curse of sin. Way back in Genesis 3, we find that because of sin, a curse was placed upon three things: the serpent, the ground (earth), and man. Man's soul was redeemed at Calvary, and his body shall be redeemed at the rapture when all the bodies of the saved shall be raised incorruptible and receive glorified bodies. After the rapture, the earth shall be redeemed during the tribulation, Daniel's seventieth week. (See Daniel 9:24,12:4-9, and Isaiah 29:9-16)

We shall look at the redemption process in a moment, but let's first finish our summary of Chapter 5. Verse 2 asks *"Who is worthy to open the book...?"* John weeps much because no man is found in heaven or earth that is worthy to open the book. John is weeping for good reason, for if the book is not opened and the earth is not redeemed, the church, which is the bride of Christ, cannot return to the earth for the

27

one thousand year reign of Christ, and the devil will have a victory. In verse 5, one of the twenty-four elders, whom we saw in Chapter 4, announces that someone has prevailed and is worthy to open the book: Revelation 5:5 *"And one of the elders saith unto me, Weep not: behold, the Lion of the tribe of Juda, the Root of David, hath prevailed to open the book, and to loose the seven seals thereof."* Of course, this is Jesus Christ Himself, and how interesting that the first time we see Jesus in John's vision of the rapture is here in Revelation 5:6 where we see Christ in the midst of the elders and the throne. We see the Trinity and also proof that it is the Father on the throne, not Jesus. (We will see Jesus on the throne in chapter 20) Revelation 5:7 *"And he came and took the book out of the right hand of him that sat upon the throne."* Jesus takes the book from the Father because He, and only He, meets the requirements of the Redeemer.

To fully understand Chapter 5 and this seven sealed book, the title deed to the earth, you need to understand the laws of the kinsman redeemer of the Old Testament. Let me briefly explain this to you so that Revelation Chapter 5 will make sense to you. A proper understanding of this chapter is important to understanding the rest of the book of Revelation.

In Genesis 3, a curse came upon the serpent, man, and all creation. Man's soul was redeemed at Calvary (I Peter 1:18,23), his body will be redeemed at the rapture (I John 3:1-2 and Romans 8:23). We know that Satan is never going to be redeemed, but what about the earth? Since we are coming back to this earth for one thousand years, it too must be redeemed. This will take place during the tribulation, and is what the opening of the seals is all about. Romans 8:22 *"For we know that the whole creation groaneth and travaileth in pain together until now."* This verse teaches that the whole world is in turmoil now because of the curse of God. (See also Genesis 3:17-19 for a reference to this curse on the earth.)

To understand the right of the Kinsman Redeemer, we need to simply look at some Old Testament examples. There are three things that could be redeemed:

1. A Wife- The brother of the deceased husband was to take his brother's wife as his own, as long as he could support her. In the allegorical sense, the church is the wife, the bride of Christ, and was redeemed at Calvary.

2. A Slave- One who could not pay his debts became a slave to his creditor for six years. Praise God, we were slaves to sin, but Romans 6:1-14 tells us we are redeemed and do not have to be a slave to sin! In fact, the new man, your spirit, that has been born again, can NOT sin!

I John 3:9 *"Whosoever is born of God doth not commit sin; for his seed remaineth in him: and he cannot sin, because he is born of God."*

Our old man, the flesh, still sins. It is the old man, the flesh, that we struggle with. This flesh will be redeemed at the rapture. So many go into false doctrine on this issue. Some claim that if we continue in sin, we are not saved, and quote a verse like I John 3:9. Yet the Bible clearly says in the same book of I John 1:8 *"If we say that we have no sin, we deceive ourselves, and the truth is not in us."* Is this a contradiction in the Bible? No, it is speaking concerning the new man, the born again part, and the old man, the flesh. Ephesians 4:22-24 *"That ye put off concerning the former conversation the old man, which is corrupt according to the deceitful lusts; And be renewed in the spirit of your mind; And that ye put on the new man, which after God is created in righteousness and true holiness."* (Also see Romans 6:6)

3. Land- Lost due to debt.

28

In the case of loss of land due to debt, the Bible teaches the law of redemption concerning property, or land. In the case of property, unlike a slave or a widow, when a person lost his property due to debt, a scroll was written up by the judges and ownership of the land was transferred to the creditor. This is kind of like a bank repossession or foreclosure in our day. However, this was not a permanent transfer in Old Testament days, as all land would go back to the original owner at the year of Jubilee. (I will not deal with that in this lesson) A document, called a scroll, would be written up. Inside that scroll would be the terms of redemption for the property. In other words, the cost of buying the land back. This scroll would then be sealed until the day a kinsman came to redeem the land, the debtor came up with the money, or the day of Jubilee, which occurs every fifty years. This document is exactly what this scroll in Revelation 5 looks like! It, too, is sealed, and it, too, contains the terms of redemption of property, the deed to all the earth, which is right now ruled by Satan. You understand that man was given dominion over the earth, until he sinned and gave up that dominion to the devil. During the tribulation, the seven sealed book will be opened and the terms of redemption of this sin-cursed world shall be revealed and fulfilled by Christ, the Kinsman Redeemer.

The book of Leviticus 25:1-55 gives us three qualifications of the one who would redeem property. This explains why none were found worthy in heaven and earth except the Lord Jesus. Let's look at these three requirements that Christ fulfilled:

1. He must be a near kinsman of the person who lost the inheritance. In Revelation 5:5 Jesus fulfilled this role. He is of the right tribe and lineage.

2. He must be able to redeem it. He must have the financial ability to redeem it. Praise the Lord, "*He owns the cattle on a thousand hills....*" And He has the power and might to wrench it from the hands of Satan! You see, the devil is not going to let it go easily as the judges would; it must be taken by force by the Lord.

3. He must be willing to redeem the property.

The kinsman did not have to redeem the land if he did not choose to (Ruth 4:1-12). But praise the Lord, Jesus is both willing and able to redeem the land. For examples of the Kinsman Redeemer, see Jeremiah 32:6-15, and book of Ruth Chapters 1-4.

So you see, for six thousand years this old earth has been owned by Satan and has been groaning and travailing under the curse of sin. We have gone through the whole Church Age in Chapters 2 and 3, the rapture has occurred in Chapter 4, and now we see the scroll in the right hand of the Father that contains the terms of the redemption of this world. Heaven and earth were searched for one who was worthy, one who met the three requirements of the kinsman redeemer, and none was found. Now you understand why John was weeping? He knew the following:

1. If the book was not opened and the earth redeemed, then all the Old Testament prophecies to be fulfilled in the Millennium would be void.

2. All creation would remain under the curse (Romans 8:22)

3. Israel would never be restored (Romans 11:1-36)

4. Many Bible promises would be unfulfilled. (Matthew 5:18)

But, praise the Lord, Jesus our Kinsman Redeemer meets the conditions, and is both willing and able to open the book and loose the seals of the book. There is great rejoicing in heaven over this event. In the next several chapters, we will see the awful terms of the redemption of this earth from the hands of Satan and from the curse of sin.

Read again Daniel 9:24 and realize that the tribulation is not about Christians or the church, but rather about the redemption of the earth to make an end of sin, to make reconciliation, to anoint the Lord Jesus as King of Kings! It has all to do with Israel. God has one final week of years to deal with them and to bring in everlasting righteousness.

I trust that this summary has helped your understanding of the purpose and reason for end time events. You may need to review this chapter some more before going on to Chapter 6, as it is important to understand.

LESSONS:

1. Notice there is weeping in heaven.

Revelation 5:4 *"And I wept much, because no man was found worthy to open and to read the book, neither to look thereon."*

You see, tears will not be wiped away until the end of the one thousand year reign of Christ and the Great White Throne judgment (See Revelation 21:4).

I wonder if there are some moms who weep in heaven over a wayward child. Maybe a child in heaven weeps over a lost parent? I do not think I have ever heard anyone preach about tears in heaven, yet it is clear that people can and do weep in heaven.

2. Prayer is important to God.

Revelation 5:8 *"And when he had taken the book, the four beasts and four and twenty elders fell down before the Lamb, having every one of them harps, and golden vials full of odours, which are the prayers of saints."*

Our prayers are so important to God that He keeps them in vials, or bottles, for remembrance.

3. Singing is an important part of worship and praise.

Revelation 5:9 *"And they sung a new song, saying, Thou art worthy to take the book, and to open the seals thereof: for thou wast slain, and hast redeemed us to God by thy blood out of every kindred, and tongue, and people, and nation;"*

We should sing more often, and we should teach our children to sing. The Psalms were the hymn book for the Israelites. *"Make a joyful noise unto the Lord."* Singing opens our spirit to the filling of God's Spirit (Ephesians 5:19).

4. Since this world is not our home, we should lay up treasure in heaven. (Matthew 6:33)

It is not our job to try to save the world, but to get people out of the world.

PERSONAL APPLICATION:

1. Ask yourself, "Is there someone weeping over me in heaven?"
2. The best thing I can do for a loved one who has died is to live for the Lord.
3. Have I any prayers in that bottle in heaven?
4. Do I know and sing good godly songs? (Ephesians 5:19)
5. Am I laying up treasure down here that will be of no value five seconds after the rapture? (Matthew 6:33)

CLOSING:

This old world is sin-cursed. What a joy to know that one day soon, we are going to be "*caught up*" as John was, and we will spend eternity with the Lord. Now let's turn our attention to Chapter 6 and see what is in store for those who miss the rapture.

REVELATION Chapter 6

THEME: THE FOUR HORSEMEN

SUMMARY:

In Chapter 1 we saw Christ's relationship to the church. In Chapters 2 and 3 we went through the entire Church Age. We saw the first century Apostolic Age represented by the church of Ephesus. We saw the church of Smyrna which represented a suffering church that took place under ten emperors of Rome from 100-313 A. D. We saw the church merge with the state under Constantine which lasted from 313-590 A. D. as represented by the church of Pergamos. Then we saw the dark ages represented by the church of Thyatira from 590-1500 A. D., where works and ceremonies had been added to the gospel. Then we saw a remnant represented by the church of Sardis from 1500-1700 as the great reformation took place under Martin Luther and others. From 1700-1901 we had the Philadelphia age of the church where many great revivals took place.

We now find the church under the sickening time of the Laodicean age where everyone wants their rights. This is the church age that makes God sick, and the age that will be here when the rapture occurs in Revelation 4. Chapters 4 and 5 took us through the rapture and the importance of the seven sealed book and Christ our Kinsman Redeemer. Now we have come to Revelation Chapter 6 and the opening of the seals which will begin the terrible judgments of the tribulation period. The seven year tribulation begins at the rapture in Chapter 4, but the actual beginning of the events on earth begin in Chapter 6, while chapters 4 and 5 gave us the events taking place in heaven at the rapture.

Are you still with me? Remember, Chapters 6-19 are the actual tribulation period. There are chapters that are inserted the middle which we call "parenthetical" chapters. In other words, they are inserted to help explain some things, to shed light on something. Apart from that, the book of Revelation is basically in order. To help you understand what I mean by a parenthetical chapter, think of a novel you may have read. Often as the story unfolds, the author will pause in the story to go back and explain a character or some event that took place in the past. That is exactly what the Lord does with these parenthetical chapters. Chapter 12 is a good example.

Now, let's look at Revelation Chapter 6. Our theme for the chapter is THE FOUR HORSEMEN, which are actually the first four seals. There are six seals opened in this chapter, but such a great emphasis is placed on these four horsemen, that I've chosen it as the theme of this chapter.

Revelation 6:1 "And I saw when the Lamb opened one of the seals, and I heard, as it were the noise of thunder, one of the four beasts saying, Come and see. 2 And I saw, and behold a white horse: and he that sat on him had a bow; and a crown was given unto him: and he went forth conquering, and to conquer. 3 And when he had opened the second seal, I heard the second beast say, Come and see. 4 And there went out another horse that was red: and power was given to him that sat thereon to take peace from the earth, and that they should kill one another: and there was given unto him a great sword. 5 And when he had opened the third seal, I heard the third beast say, Come and see. And I beheld, and lo a black horse;

32

and he that sat on him had a pair of balances in his hand.
6 And I heard a voice in the midst of the four beasts say, A measure of wheat for a penny, and three measures of barley for a penny; and see thou hurt not the oil and the wine. 7 And when he had opened the fourth seal, I heard the voice of the fourth beast say, Come and see. 8 And I looked, and behold a pale horse: and his name that sat on him was Death, and Hell followed with him. And power was given unto them over the fourth part of the earth, to kill with sword, and with hunger, and with death, and with the beasts of the earth."

Verse 1 lets us know it is the Lord Jesus Himself Who begins these events. That does not mean He causes them, but rather He sets them in motion.

NOTE: As we study Chapters 6-19, you will find that the first set of seven judgments, the seven seals, are basically caused by man through wars. The second set of judgments, the seven trumpets at the middle of the tribulation, are instigated by Satan's wrath after he is cast out of heaven and restricted to earth. The third and most severe judgments, the seven vials, are the wrath of God upon this earth near the end of the seven years. Notice they get more severe as time goes on. Notice the most severe judgment comes from the Lord.

THE WHITE HORSE in verse 2 is the antichrist. Do not confuse him with the Lord on the white horse in Revelation 19:11. Notice that the antichrist has a bow but no arrows. I believe this signifies that he will rule without making war at his arrival. In fact, the verse says "*a crown was given unto him.*" I believe the world will be in such chaos after the rapture, with planes crashing, people missing, car wrecks on every highway, that the world will be looking for someone with answers to the world's problems. The false christ will have those answers, and he will be promoted to power over the world. Then "*he went forth conquering and to conquer.*" This leads to THE RED HORSE in verses 3-4 which is the second seal. Notice he has power given to him to take peace from the world and he is given a great sword. Maybe it will be the armies of the United Nations that are under his authority. Many will die in these wars, but keep in mind that Israel will not be at war, but will be in a peace agreement with the antichrist (See Daniel 9:27). The whole world, except for Israel, will be at war. At the middle of the tribulation, in the midst of the week (after three and one-half years), the antichrist sits in the temple and declares he is God. He declares war on the Jews, and then the Great Tribulation, the time of "Jacob's Trouble" begins (See II Thessalonians 2:3-4 and Matthew 24:15-22).

Now, these worldwide wars will lead to:

THE BLACK HORSE in verses 5-6, the opening of the third seal. This is worldwide famine, a normal result of wars. The rich will be the only ones who are not harmed by this famine, those with the oil and the wine. (This could also refer to the one hundred forty-four thousand sealed Jews) This famine leads to:

THE PALE HORSE in verses 7-8, the opening of the 4th seal. This is death, and hell follows him. There is nobody saved as yet; therefore everyone who dies during the first half of the tribulation goes to hell. Millions will die from war, starvation, and disease. The mark of the beast has not yet come into effect, and there are not any saved people to be martyred. The mark of the beast and the salvation of the one hundred forty-four thousand Jews take place in the second half of the tribulation.

The one hundred forty-four thousand Jews will be the first fruits, the first people saved during the tribulation (Revelation 14:1-4), but not until the antichrist enters the temple at the middle of the tribulation. He will declare himself to be God, break his peace treaty with Israel, and kill the two witnesses, probably Moses and Elijah, who after three and one-half days arise and ascend to heaven. It is then that the one hundred forty-four thousand get saved and flee from the antichrist. I believe a reference to their salvation is Revelation 11:13. They become God's missionaries and lead many to salvation during the second half of the tribulation.

The fifth seal in Revelation 6:9 talks about the martyrs in heaven. In verse 10 these martyrs are asking how long until they are avenged. Verse 11 is the key as to who they are: "*And white robes were given unto every one of them; and it was said unto them, that they should rest yet for a little season, until their fellowservants also and their brethren, that should be killed as they were, should be fulfilled.* It is clear that the saints we see in verse 9 at the opening of the fifth seal are church age martyrs, NOT tribulation martyrs. First, there is nobody saved during the first half. Second, why would they be crying out "How long?" if they had just been there a few months or days? The "fellowservants" in verse 11 are the tribulation martyrs. Remember what the tribulation is about? It is the redeeming of the earth, the making an end of sin. The avenging of the death of these church age saints is part of this redemption process, thus we see this in the opening of the fifth seal, as well as the promise of more martyrs to come.

The sixth seal is opened in Revelation 6:12 and seems to be nuclear war, or some other earth shaking event. Nuclear bombs certainly shake the earth, and the smoke conceals the sun and stars. It is interesting, even shocking, that the people on the earth seek to hide from God rather than trust Jesus for salvation. Revelation 6:15-17 "*And the kings of the earth, and the great men, and the rich men, and the chief captains, and the mighty men, and every bondman, and every free man, hid themselves in the dens and in the rocks of the mountains; And said to the mountains and rocks, Fall on us, and hide us from the face of him that sitteth on the throne, and from the wrath of the Lamb: For the great day of his wrath is come; and who shall be able to stand?*"

Do not confuse this event with the second coming, as this is right before the middle of the tribulation.

Chapter 7, which we shall study next, is one of those parenthetical chapters we discussed earlier. A chapter inserted to make some things more clear, similar to a sentence with a phrase set off by parenthesis. The sentence will stand alone, but the phrase gives you a better understanding. 2 Peter 2:7-8 "*And delivered just Lot, vexed with the filthy conversation of the wicked: (For that righteous man dwelling among them, in seeing and hearing, vexed his righteous soul from day to day with their unlawful deeds....)*" This is exactly what a parenthetical chapter is, a pause to help the reader understand some things. Revelation Chapter 7 is such a chapter; it is placed between the sixth and seventh seals. The seventh seal is opened in Chapter 8 and is the middle of the tribulation.

LESSONS:

1. Think of these four horsemen as events, not men.
I realize the first horseman represents the false christ, but think of it rather as an

event. It is the crowning of a world dictator, the antichrist. Each of the seals, trumpet judgments, etc., are events that will take place.

2. The opening of the next seal, or the blowing of another trumpet, does not end the prior judgment, but rather adds to it.
In other words, when a destructive earthquake takes place in one of the judgments, soon another judgment takes place and the attention is drawn away, but remember that there is still the awful suffering and chaos from the earthquake that has taken place! The new judgment does not end the prior judgment, but adds to it.

3. One-fourth of the world's population that is here after the rapture will die in the first four seals alone. Remember, all those who die in the first half die lost and go to hell.

4. Realize, it is Jesus who opens the seals and begins this terrible time of tribulation.

5. The judgments of the tribulation are the process of redemption for this sin-cursed world, and for the nation of Israel.

PERSONAL APPLICATION:
1. Be sure you are saved.
2. Do all you can to get your loved ones saved.
3. Live your life like you believe Christ could return today!

CLOSING: Thank God for the "Blessed Hope" of Titus 2:13, *"Looking for that blessed hope, and the glorious appearing of the great God and our Saviour Jesus Christ...."*

REVELATION CHAPTER 7

THEME: THE SEALED ONE HUNDRED FORTY-FOUR THOUSAND
(A Parenthetical Chapter)

SUMMARY:

In Chapter 1, we saw Christ and His relationship to His church. In Chapters 2 and 3 we have gone through the whole Church Age, and then the rapture in Chapter 4. We see in Chapter 5 that the Lamb of God, Jesus, has prevailed, and has taken the seven sealed book, the title deed to the earth, out of the Father's hand. In Chapter 6 He has begun opening the seals, beginning the tribulation period, and revealing the redemption process of the earth and Israel. We ended Chapter 6 with the sixth seal.

Revelation 7:1 "And after these things I saw four angels standing on the four corners of the earth, holding the four winds of the earth, that the wind should not blow on the earth, nor on the sea, nor on any tree. 2 And I saw another angel ascending from the east, having the seal of the living God: and he cried with a loud voice to the four angels, to whom it was given to hurt the earth and the sea, 3 Saying, Hurt not the earth, neither the sea, nor the trees, until we have sealed the servants of our God in their foreheads. 4 And I heard the number of them which were sealed: and there were sealed an hundred and forty and four thousand of all the tribes of the children of Israel. 5 Of the tribe of Juda were sealed twelve thousand. Of the tribe of Reuben were sealed twelve thousand. Of the tribe of Gad were sealed twelve thousand. 6 Of the tribe of Aser were sealed twelve thousand. Of the tribe of Nepthalim were sealed twelve thousand. Of the tribe of Manasses were sealed twelve thousand. 7 Of the tribe of Simeon were sealed twelve thousand. Of the tribe of Levi were sealed twelve thousand. Of the tribe of Issachar were sealed twelve thousand. 8 Of the tribe of Zabulon were sealed twelve thousand. Of the tribe of Joseph were sealed twelve thousand. Of the tribe of Benjamin were sealed twelve thousand. 9 After this I beheld, and, lo, a great multitude, which no man could number, of all nations, and kindreds, and people, and tongues, stood before the throne, and before the Lamb, clothed with white robes, and palms in their hands; 10 And cried with a loud voice, saying, Salvation to our God which sitteth upon the throne, and unto the Lamb. 11 And all the angels stood round about the throne, and about the elders and the four beasts, and fell before the throne on their faces, and worshipped God, 12 Saying, Amen: Blessing, and glory, and wisdom, and thanksgiving, and honour, and power, and might, be unto our God for ever and ever. Amen. 13 And one of the elders answered, saying unto me, What are these which are arrayed in white robes? and whence came they? 14 And I said unto him, Sir, thou knowest. And he said to me, These are they which came out of great tribulation, and have washed their robes, and made them white in the blood of the Lamb. 15 Therefore are they before the throne of God, and serve him day and night in his temple: and he that sitteth on the throne shall dwell among them. 16 They shall hunger no more, neither thirst any more; neither shall the sun light on them, nor any heat. 17 For the Lamb which is in the midst of the throne shall feed them, and shall lead them unto living fountains of waters: and God shall wipe away all tears from their eyes."

This brings us to the discussion of the "sealed one hundred forty-four thousand" in Revelation Chapter 7, which is a parenthetical chapter. We discussed what we mean by "parenthetical" previously, it is a chapter inserted to explain some things either past, present, or future to help shed light on a truth. Notice this chapter is inserted between the sixth and seventh seals.

Chapter 7 comes after we have just read the sobering account of possibly one billion people dying and going to hell. Chapter 7 is inserted between these two seals to let us know that as bad as things seem, there is going to be some good come out of all this.

36

There are one hundred forty-four thousand sealed from the twelve tribes, Hebrews, or Jews if you will, who are protected by God and are going to be the first folks saved during the tribulation (Revelation 11:13, 14:1-4) .

A seal represents ownership and Lordship, as a king's seal. A seal also represents protection, as a trucking company will place a seal on the doors of a trailer to protect from theft. A seal also shows identity. Christ places his seal upon us (Ephesians 1:13, 4:30).

God is letting us know that no matter how bad the tribulation gets, these one hundred forty-four thousand are protected by God, and are saved at the middle of the tribulation. It is these saved one hundred forty-four thousand that lead in the salvation of countless people during the second half, many of whom will be martyred. Revelation 7:9 *"After this I beheld, and, lo, a great multitude, which no man could number, of all nations, and kindreds, and people, and tongues, stood before the throne, and before the Lamb, clothed with white robes, and palms in their hands;"*

Verses 13-17 are future events. It is a bit humorous if you think about it. John, by way of a vision in Chapter 4, is seeing the future, and while seeing the future, he is shown the next future! In other words, in verse 9 he is shown a future event that is going to take place, and then in verses 13-17 one of the elders shows him something even further into the future.

Revelation 7:13 "And one of the elders answered, saying unto me, What are these which are arrayed in white robes? and whence came they? And I said unto him, Sir, thou knowest. And he said to me, These are they which came out of <u>great tribulation,</u> and have washed their robes, and made them white in the blood of the Lamb. Therefore are they before the throne of God, and serve him day and night in his temple: and he that sitteth on the throne shall dwell among them. They shall hunger no more, neither thirst any more; neither shall the sun light on them, nor any heat. For the Lamb which is in the midst of the throne shall feed them, and shall lead them unto living fountains of waters: and God shall wipe away all tears from their eyes."

In these last verses, John is seeing people who were saved during the "great tribulation," the second half of the seven years. See verse 14 above. These are the future martyrs that the church age martyrs were to wait for in Revelation 6:10-11.

LESSONS:

1. God is in complete control of the events of the tribulation. Revelation 7:3, *"Saying, Hurt not the earth, neither the sea, nor the trees, until we have sealed the servants of our God in their foreheads."*

Nothing ever catches God by surprise. God has never had to say "oops." The tribulation will unfold according to His plan.

2. The one hundred forty-four thousand are Jews, not Jehovah's Witnesses, or Gentiles. It is plain as day in the text.

3. We, too, have been sealed by God.
Ephesians 1:13-14 "In whom ye also trusted, after that ye heard the word of truth, the gospel of your salvation: in whom also after that ye believed, ye were sealed with that holy Spirit of promise, Which is the earnest of our inheritance until the redemption of the purchased possession, unto the praise of his glory." Ephesians 4:30 "And grieve not the holy Spirit of God, whereby ye are <u>sealed</u> unto the day of redemption."

Remember this seal implies ownership and protection. People who want to fight the doctrine of eternal security just have not "*rightly divided*" the Scriptures. Ephesians 1:13-14 explains that the Holy Spirit is the down payment, the assurance money if you will, for the purchased possession, our souls. Once I have trusted Christ, if I die and go to hell, the Holy Spirit would have to go with me. The old timers know what earnest money means. It is the down payment they would apply to secure a transaction until they could gather up the remaining price of the property. If for any reason they did not have the balance by closing day, they forfeited the earnest money. So you see, God has given His Holy Spirit as earnest money, or a guarantee of His desire to fulfill the contract, until we get to heaven. Look at it in Ephesians 1:14 *"Which is the earnest of our inheritance until the redemption of the purchased possession, unto the praise of his glory."*
4. Praise the Lord, Revelation 7:14-17 lets us know that the day is coming that we will suffer no more and will dwell with the Lord forever!

PERSONAL APPLICATION:
1. Have I the complete assurance that I am eternally secure in Christ?
   I John 5:13, John 10:28-29, Hebrews 7:25, 13:5
2. Am I standing for Jesus through the tribulations and trials of this life?
3. Do I look for the hand of God in the happenings of life?

CLOSING:
We have now covered nearly all of the first half of the tribulation. As bad as it is, the worst is yet to come. If you're not 100% sure of your salvation, be sure to get help, and see the last chapter of this guide. If you are sure of salvation, take a moment and thank God for His mercy.

REVELATION Chapter 8

THEME: A PAUSE IN HEAVEN
(Middle of Tribulation, half-time)

SUMMARY:

In Revelation Chapter 1, we saw Christ in the midst of the churches. In Chapters 2 and 3 we saw the whole age of church history pass before our eyes. Chapter 4 is the rapture of all the believers on earth and a glimpse of what goes on in heaven at that time. In Chapter 5 the seven sealed book, the title deed to the earth, is taken by Christ, and He begins to open those seals in Chapter 6. Chapter 7 is a parenthesis in the story, and we see that one hundred forty-four thousand Jews are going to be saved later. Many will be martyred and join the church age martyrs that we saw in Revelation 6:9.

Now we come to Chapter 8, where we see silence in heaven for half an hour. It is probably "half-time." In other words, the first three and one-half years of the tribulation are over, and the second half, the "Great Tribulation" begins. This time is called "The Time of Jacob's Trouble." Now I cannot be 100% certain that this is "half-time," but I am certain that the three woes, which are the last three trumpets that sound in Chapter 9 are the second half, the Great Tribulation. I believe that the second half begins after the silence in heaven in Chapter 8:1, and that the first four trumpets sound very quickly ushering in the three woes of Chapter 9 which are definitely the second half. During this time, Satan is cast to the earth, defiles the temple, ends the sacrifices, and breaks his treaty with Israel. This leads to the one hundred forty-four thousand getting saved, probably after seeing the two witnesses raise from the dead. Are you with me so far? Stay with me, we shall look at the two witnesses and the salvation of the one hundred forty-four thousand later in Chapters 11 and 14. Now let's look at the text:

Revelation 8:1-6 "And when he had opened the seventh seal, there was <u>silence in heaven about the space of half an hour.</u> And I saw the seven angels which stood before God; and to them were given seven trumpets. And another angel came and stood at the altar, having a golden censer; and there was given unto him much incense, that he should offer it with the prayers of all saints upon the golden altar which was before the throne. And the smoke of the incense, which came with the prayers of the saints, ascended up before God out of the angel's hand. And the angel took the censer, and filled it with fire of the altar, and cast it into the earth: and there were voices, and thunderings, and lightnings, and an earthquake. And the seven angels which had the seven trumpets prepared themselves to sound."

Notice that I underlined the part about silence for half an hour. The first thing I think of here is a sporting event. At the middle of the game, both teams head for the locker room for a short break. I believe that the opening of the seventh seal is right at the middle of the tribulation, and, after a short pause, the second half begins with seven angels revealed, each with a trumpet to sound. Each of these trumpets is a judgment, and all seven make up the seventh seal. In verses 7-13 you see the first four trumpets sounding. These seem to be earth related judgments of hail, trees burned up, water turned to blood, falling stars, and the sun and moon seem darkened, probably from smoke. I believe these first four trumpets blow one after another very quickly. These sound very much like the judgments God brought upon Egypt through Moses. Some believe that the star that falls in verse 10 is actually a fallen angel. This may or may not be true, but it is always best to take the Bible literally unless the context shows differently, therefore I believe this is not an angel. It is interesting to note though, that Revelation 9:1 speaks of a fallen angel as a fallen star, but the context there plainly shows us that it is Satan, and we shall look at that in the next chapter.

Now look at Revelation 8:13 *"And I beheld, and heard an angel flying through the midst of heaven, saying with a loud voice, Woe, woe, woe, to the inhabiters of the earth by reason of the other voices of the trumpet of the three angels, which are yet to sound!"*

A stern warning is given concerning these three woes. The last three trumpets are called the three woes to emphasize their horror. These are the "beginning of sorrows" for Israel, and are the second half of the tribulation as seen in Matthew 24. We shall look at these in the next chapter.

It would be helpful in your study to highlight each of the seven seals, trumpets, and vials in your Bible so you can find them easily.

LESSONS:

1. Notice it is silence in heaven, not earth. There is no break in the events of the tribulation. (Revelation 8:1)

2. We see again how important the prayers of the saints are to God. (Revelation 8:4)

3. In Revelation 8:5 we see thunder and lightning, which tells us that a storm is on the way from God!

4. In Revelation 8:13 we see that the worst is yet to come! *"And I beheld, and heard an angel flying through the midst of heaven, saying with a loud voice, Woe, woe, woe, to the inhabiters of the earth by reason of the other voices of the trumpet of the three angels, which are yet to sound!"*

PERSONAL APPLICATION:

1. Now is the time for God's people to send prayers to heaven! My prayers DO matter to God!
2. Do I have some loved ones still unsaved?
3. Will some friends or family of mine be present for the three woes spoken of here? Take a few minutes and let this sink in.

CLOSING: With the close of Chapter 8, we now turn our attention to the three woes of Chapter 9. Remember, Chapter 8 continues where we left off in Chapter 6 with the opening of the sixth seal. Chapter 7 was a parenthetical chapter inserted to explain some things.

REVELATION Chapter 9

THEME: HELL ON EARTH

SUMMARY:
In Chapter 1, we saw Christ in the midst of the seven golden candlesticks. In Chapters 2 and 3 we saw the seven letters written to the seven churches, and we clearly see that these seven churches have a prophetic meaning. We see that they represent seven ages of church history. You and I are living in the last age, the Laodicean Age. One of these days the trumpet will sound and we shall be taken to heaven, as we saw in Chapter 4; it is the next event on God's calendar. The opening of the seals takes place in Chapter 6 by Christ Himself. We saw the antichrist rise to power, we saw wars and famines and death in the first four seals as at least a billion people died and went to hell. We left off at the end of Chapter 8 with a warning concerning the last three trumpets, the three woes. We shall now look at Chapter 9.

Revelation 9:1 "And the fifth angel sounded, and I saw a star fall from heaven unto the earth: and to him was given the key of the bottomless pit.
2 And he opened the bottomless pit; and there arose a smoke out of the pit, as the smoke of a great furnace; and the sun and the air were darkened by reason of the smoke of the pit.
3 And there came out of the smoke locusts upon the earth: and unto them was given power, as the scorpions of the earth have power.
4 And it was commanded them that they should not hurt the grass of the earth, neither any green thing, neither any tree; but only those men which have not the seal of God in their foreheads.
5 And to them it was given that they should not kill them, but that they should be tormented five months: and their torment was as the torment of a scorpion, when he striketh a man.
6 And in those days shall men seek death, and shall not find it; and shall desire to die, and death shall flee from them.
7 And the shapes of the locusts were like unto horses prepared unto battle; and on their heads were as it were crowns like gold, and their faces were as the faces of men.
8 And they had hair as the hair of women, and their teeth were as the teeth of lions.
9 And they had breastplates, as it were breastplates of iron; and the sound of their wings was as the sound of chariots of many horses running to battle.
10 And they had tails like unto scorpions, and there were stings in their tails: and their power was to hurt men five months.
11 And they had a king over them, which is the angel of the bottomless pit, whose name in the Hebrew tongue is Abaddon, but in the Greek tongue hath his name Apollyon.
12 One woe is past; and, behold, there come two woes more hereafter.
13 And the sixth angel sounded, and I heard a voice from the four horns of the golden altar which is before God,
14 Saying to the sixth angel which had the trumpet, Loose the four angels which are bound in the great river Euphrates.
15 And the four angels were loosed, which were prepared for an hour, and a day, and a month, and a year, for to slay the third part of men.
16 And the number of the army of the horsemen were two hundred thousand thousand: and I heard the number of them.
17 And thus I saw the horses in the vision, and them that sat on them, having breastplates of fire, and of jacinth, and brimstone: and the heads of the horses were as the heads of lions; and out of their mouths

issued fire and smoke and brimstone.

18 By these three was the third part of men killed, by the fire, and by the smoke, and by the brimstone, which issued out of their mouths.

19 For their power is in their mouth, and in their tails: for their tails were like unto serpents, and had heads, and with them they do hurt.

20 And the rest of the men which were not killed by these plagues yet repented not of the works of their hands, that they should not worship devils, and idols of gold, and silver, and brass, and stone, and of wood: which neither can see, nor hear, nor walk:

21 Neither repented they of their murders, nor of their sorceries, nor of their fornication, nor of their thefts."

I call this chapter "Hell On Earth" because here Satan is cast out of heaven and given the keys to the bottomless pit. He releases the demons from the pit to torment men for five months. This takes place at the fifth trumpet, also called the first woe. We see this in verses 1-12. This torment will be so bad that men will try to end their lives, but will not be able to (verse 6). We see that these "locust" have a king over them, and he is Satan himself as seen in verse 11.

The sixth trumpet, the second woe, is opened in verses 13-21. We see that one-third of the population will die, and that even after this, men will still not repent (Revelation 9:20-21)! Read 2 Thessalonians 2:10-12 for the likely reason why: *"And with all deceivableness of unrighteousness in them that perish; because they received not the love of the truth, that they might be saved. And for this cause God shall send them strong delusion, that they should believe a lie: That they all might be damned who believed not the truth, but had pleasure in unrighteousness."*

You see, people who have heard and rejected Christ before the rapture, will not get a second chance after the rapture. (See page 81 for more on this subject.)

What a terrible time this will be! Satan, because he is kicked out of heaven (Revelation 12:6-13), will realize he has but a short time and so will release the demons from the pit (Revelation 9:1); move Antichrist to enter the temple in Jerusalem, end the temple sacrifices, declare he is God (Matthew 24:15, 2 Thessalonians 2:4, Daniel 9:27); break the peace treaty with Israel, and then kill the two prophets and leave their bodies in the streets for three and one-half days. After this, the two prophets arise and ascend to heaven (see Revelation 11), and then the one hundred forty-four thousand get saved (Revelation 11:13), and become the first converts during the tribulation. See Revelation 14:4: *"These are they which were not defiled with women; for they are virgins. These are they which follow the Lamb whithersoever he goeth. These were redeemed from among men, being the firstfruits unto God and to the Lamb."*

These "firstfruits," the first people saved during the tribulation, will flee from the Antichrist and lead many to salvation. Most of them will be martyred during the tribulation. This second half is called the "Great Tribulation", the time of Jacob's trouble. Look what Matthew 24:21-22 says of this time: *"For then shall be great tribulation, such as was not since the beginning of the world to this time, no, nor ever shall be. And except those days should be shortened, there should no flesh be saved: but for the elect's sake those days shall be shortened."*

LESSONS:

1. The star that fell in Revelation 9:1 is Satan at the middle of the tribulation. When we read Chapters 1 and 2 of Job, we see that Satan has access to God and is the "accuser of the Brethren."

Revelation 12:10, *"And I heard a loud voice saying in heaven, Now is come salvation, and strength, and the kingdom of our God, and the power of his Christ: for the accuser of our brethren is cast down, which accused them before our God day and night."*

2. Satan is thrown out of heaven at the middle of the tribulation. (Revelation 12:7-13)

3. This leads to the increased wrath of Satan upon those on the earth, and especially the Jews. I call it "Hell on Earth." Satan is given the key to the bottomless pit in Revelation 9:1 and leads these demons on a rampage of the earth.

4. The judgments get worse and worse as the tribulation unfolds. We saw the results caused by man in the first seals, now we see the wrath of Satan in the trumpet judgments. When we get to the seven vials, we will see that the wrath of God is worse yet!

5. It is the restraining power of the Holy Spirit in the believers that now holds back the forces of the devil and his demons. 2 Thessalonians 2:6-8 *"And now ye know what withholdeth that he might be revealed in his time. For the mystery of iniquity doth already work: only he who now letteth will let, until he be taken out of the way. And then shall that Wicked be revealed, whom the Lord shall consume with the spirit of his mouth, and shall destroy with the brightness of his coming:"*

PERSONAL APPLICATION:
1. Realize, no matter how bad things may get for you in this life, you don't have it so bad when compared to the tribulation.
2. Have you ever considered that some people you love dearly may go through this terrible time unless you win them to Christ?
3. Is there some sin in your life that you have refused to repent of, as those in Revelation 9:20-21?

CLOSING: We have just finished a very sobering chapter in the Bible. Thank God for His saving grace! Aren't you glad you do not have to go through this terrible time? Take a moment and thank the Lord for it, and spend some time praying for and witnessing to your loved ones.

REVELATION Chapter 10

THEME: JESUS AND THE LITTLE BOOK

SUMMARY:

Revelation 10:1 "And I saw another mighty angel come down from heaven, clothed with a cloud: and a rainbow was upon his head, and his face was as it were the sun, and his feet as pillars of fire:

2 And he had in his hand a little book open: and he set his right foot upon the sea, and his left foot on the earth,

3 And cried with a loud voice, as when a lion roareth: and when he had cried, seven thunders uttered their voices.

4 And when the seven thunders had uttered their voices, I was about to write: and I heard a voice from heaven saying unto me, Seal up those things which the seven thunders uttered, and write them not.

5 And the angel which I saw stand upon the sea and upon the earth lifted up his hand to heaven,

6 And sware by him that liveth for ever and ever, who created heaven, and the things that therein are, and the earth, and the things that therein are, and the sea, and the things which are therein, that there should be time no longer:

7 But in the days of the voice of the seventh angel, when he shall begin to sound, the mystery of God should be finished, as he hath declared to his servants the prophets.

8 And the voice which I heard from heaven spake unto me again, and said, Go and take the little book which is open in the hand of the angel which standeth upon the sea and upon the earth.

9 And I went unto the angel, and said unto him, Give me the little book. And he said unto me, Take it, and eat it up; and it shall make thy belly bitter, but it shall be in thy mouth sweet as honey.

10 And I took the little book out of the angel's hand, and ate it up; and it was in my mouth sweet as honey: and as soon as I had eaten it, my belly was bitter.

11 And he said unto me, Thou must prophesy again before many peoples, and nations, and tongues, and kings."

We left off with Chapter 9 at the sounding of the sixth trumpet, which was the second woe. Remember, the seventh seal in Revelation 8:1 is the seven trumpet judgments, and we learn from Revelation 9:13 that the fifth, sixth, and seventh trumpets are called the three woes because of their severity. The sixth trumpet which is the second woe, sounded in Revelation 9:13. There is one trumpet yet to sound, which is the third woe. We will not see it until Revelation 11:15.

Chapter 10 through Chapter 11:14 are parenthetical. They are inserted to explain some things. As I said earlier, chapters 7, 10,11,12,13, and14 are all, but for a few verses, parenthetical, and are not in chronological order. Misunderstanding this is a cause of much of the wrong teaching about Revelation. I believe the mighty angel in Revelation 10:1 is Jesus, and the book in His hand is the title deed to the earth, the judgments that you and I are reading about right now in the book of Revelation. We saw Christ with this very book in His hand in Chapter 5 and 6. We are not told what the seven thunders are, so I will not even try to guess at their meaning. In verse 6, we see that soon there will be no more time, as in reality, time is measured by decay, and there will be no decay in heaven. Verse 7 is speaking of the seventh trumpet that will be sounded in Revelation 11:15 which includes the seven vials of the wrath of God and that ends the tribulation at the battle of Armageddon and the second coming of Christ in Revelation 19:11. In verses 9-11 John is told to eat the little book which is symbolic of God's people reading and absorbing the Scriptures. Consider this: Prophecy is sweet to the taste, but it should make us sick to dwell upon.

LESSONS:

1. I am convinced the angel is Jesus because of the description given in the chapter. Compare this description to that given of Christ in Revelation 1:7 as well as his characteristics in Revelation 2 and 3. Also, we saw Him with a book in His hand in Chapter 5. His feet on the land and sea, and His voice as a lion, the rainbow, as well as the fact that He "*sware by him that liveth forever and ever...*" in verse 6 proves without a doubt that this is Jesus. Hebrews 6:13 *"For when God made promise to Abraham, because he could swear by no greater, he sware by himself...."*

2. John was not allowed to write about the seven thunders in verse 4. Maybe it was such a vivid and perverted thing, God did not want it written.

3. Verse 7 is telling of the seventh trumpet, which is the third woe, and includes the rest of the tribulation until Christ returns.

4. John is told to consume the book of prophecy so that he could preach it to future generations of people. He did so, as you and I are reading what he said. (Revelation 10:9-11)

PERSONAL APPLICATION:

1. We must receive the Word of God before we can transfer it to others.
2. It is vital that we have the Word of God, and not man's watered down version of what God said. I am a 1611 King James Bible believer! I do not like people trying to mess with God's Word! Do you have the perfect and inspired Words?
Look up these verses concerning the Scriptures:

Matthew 4:4	Matthew 24:35	Psalm 19	Psalm 12:6-7
Romans 10:17	Hebrews 4:12	John 1:1	Proverbs 30:5

3. Remember how sweet to your taste the Bible was when you first got saved? Is the Bible still sweet to you today? Psalm 19:10 *"More to be desired are they than gold, yea, than much fine gold: sweeter also than honey and the honeycomb."*
4. Some of the Bible is very bitter, but necessary.

It is a shame so many preachers refuse to preach on certain subjects for fear of offending their congregation. Let me ask you something, would you want to have a doctor who refused to tell you about your heart condition? You would be angry if he hid the facts from you. Would you want to have a lawyer who lied and said everything would be fine, or do you want a lawyer who is honest with you? Yet, so many Christians get upset with the preacher for telling them the truth about *their* heart condition! And worse than that, so many preachers are spineless and refuse to tell their church the truth.

CLOSING: Let me give you just ONE example of how the new versions (perversions) have corrupted God's Word. Look at what the 1611 King James Bible says in John 7:8-

10, *"Go ye up unto this feast: I go not up yet unto this feast; for my time is not yet full come. When he had said these words unto them, he abode still in Galilee. But when his brethren were gone up, then went he also up unto the feast, not openly, but as it were in secret."*

In some of the newer versions, the word "YET" has been left out. You may be thinking, what is the big deal about that little word "YET?" Well, to leave it out makes our Lord a liar! See, if you leave out that word, then Jesus said he was NOT going to the feast, but in verse 10 we see that He did go to the feast.

My friend, every word in the Bible is there on purpose! Do not fall for the devil's lies concerning the originals being perfect, and our English Bible being just a translation. If you want a recommendation of some good books to read on this subject, call or e-mail me and I will be glad to help you.

REVELATION Chapter 11

THEME: THE TWO WITNESSES

SUMMARY:

We have seen Christ revealed in every chapter thus far. It is after all, the Revelation or unveiling of Christ, is it not? We saw him revealed in the midst of the churches in Chapter 1. We saw Him revealed to us in each of the seven ages of church history in Chapters 2 and 3, and we saw Him call all the saved home in the rapture in Chapter 4. In Chapter 5 He was revealed as the one found worthy to take the book and loose the seals thereof and begin the tribulation period. In Chapter 6, Christ was revealed opening the seals as the four horsemen come on the scene. In chapter 7 we saw that Christ is the lamb who washes us in His blood, and will one day wipe away all our tears. In Chapter 8 He was revealed opening the seventh seal at the middle of the tribulation, and in Chapter 9 we saw that Christ kicked Satan from heaven and gave permission for him to loose some demons making it a hell on earth. In Chapter 10 we saw Christ clothed with a cloud, with His face as the sun, with feet as pillars of fire. We saw Christ give the little book to John to eat, symbolic of consuming the Word of God and sharing it with others. We now come to Chapter 11, the theme of which is "The Two Witnesses."

Revelation 11:1 "And there was given me a reed like unto a rod: and the angel stood, saying, Rise, and measure the temple of God, and the altar, and them that worship therein.
2 But the court which is without the temple leave out, and measure it not; for it is given unto the Gentiles: and the holy city shall they tread under foot forty and two months.
3 And I will give power unto my two witnesses, and they shall prophesy a thousand two hundred and threescore days, clothed in sackcloth.
4 These are the two olive trees, and the two candlesticks standing before the God of the earth.
5 And if any man will hurt them, fire proceedeth out of their mouth, and devoureth their enemies: and if any man will hurt them, he must in this manner be killed.
6 These have power to shut heaven, that it rain not in the days of their prophecy: and have power over waters to turn them to blood, and to smite the earth with all plagues, as often as they will.
7 And when they shall have finished their testimony, the beast that ascendeth out of the bottomless pit shall make war against them, and shall overcome them, and kill them.
8 And their dead bodies shall lie in the street of the great city, which spiritually is called Sodom and Egypt, where also our Lord was crucified.
9 And they of the people and kindreds and tongues and nations shall see their dead bodies three days and an half, and shall not suffer their dead bodies to be put in graves.
10 And they that dwell upon the earth shall rejoice over them, and make merry, and shall send gifts one to another; because these two prophets tormented them that dwelt on the earth.
11 And after three days and an half the Spirit of life from God entered into them, and they stood upon their feet; and great fear fell upon them which saw them.
12 And they heard a great voice from heaven saying unto them, Come up hither. And they ascended up to heaven in a cloud; and their enemies beheld them.
13 And the same hour was there a great earthquake, and the tenth part of the city fell, and in the earthquake were slain of men seven thousand: and the remnant were affrighted, and gave glory to the God of heaven.
14 The second woe is past; and, behold, the third woe cometh quickly."

Chapter 11 is another of the parenthetical chapters. It is inserted to explain some things. Remember, if you do not understand what a parenthetical chapter is, you will never get the timeline for Revelation. Go back to the introduction of this guide and refresh your memory if you need to.

Let me help you understand this chapter that is so misunderstood by so many. The chapter is going back to the beginning of the tribulation to explain something important that has been going on. Verses 1 and 2 let us know that the attention after the rapture is on the Jews, not the church (Daniel 9:24). Remember, the church is in heaven, for there are no Christians left on the earth after Revelation 4:1. The measuring of the temple lets us know that the Jews, after the rapture, will begin their Old Testament temple sacrifices again, and the rod symbolizes the judgment to come upon them. The temple will either be rebuilt just prior to or right after the rapture. It is to be built on the very spot where the Muslim Dome of the Rock is now. You have surely seen pictures of this or seen it in the news. It is a big gold-colored, dome-shaped building. It sits on holy ground, the very spot on which the new temple will be built. I look for something to happen to the Dome soon. (There are those who believe the Dome is not in the way of the Temple Mount.) This revival of Old Testament temple worship is not a good thing, for it pictures a coming Messiah rather than a crucified and risen Messiah.

Revelation 11:2 lets us know that though Israel has the temple sacrifices going again, the Gentiles are all around them. The Antichrist is going to make a peace treaty with Israel right after the rapture. As we find in Daniel 9:26-27,

"And after threescore and two weeks shall Messiah be cut off, but not for himself: and the people of the prince that shall come shall destroy the city and the sanctuary; and the end thereof shall be with a flood, and unto the end of the war desolations are determined. 27 And he shall confirm the covenant with many for one week: and in the midst of the week he shall cause the sacrifice and the oblation to cease, and for the overspreading of abominations he shall make it desolate, even until the consummation, and that determined shall be poured upon the desolate."

Do you see how important the book of Daniel is to the understanding of Revelation, especially Daniel Chapter 9? "Messiah cut off" speaks of Calvary; "the prince that shall come" is the Antichrist, the same person that is referred to in verse 27. He, the Antichrist, will confirm the covenant, make a treaty with Israel for one week, which is seven years. But right in the middle of the week of seven years, he puts an end to the temple sacrifices, goes into the temple himself and declares he is God (Matthew 24:15-21), and demands Israel worship him. This proves that Israel is going to resume the temple worship during the first half of the Tribulation. I believe that all this happens just as Satan is kicked out of heaven in Revelation Chapter 9, and the demons from the pit are loosed here on earth. I also believe this is the moment the Jews realize the truth about the gospel and the one hundred forty-four thousand get saved. I also believe this takes place at Passover. All this ushers in the second half of the Tribulation, called "The Great Tribulation" in Matthew 24:21. It is referred to as "the time of Jacob's trouble," because it is Satan warring against the Jews (Revelation 12:12-13).

Revelation 11:3-14 deal with the theme of this chapter, the two witnesses. They are called olive trees, and candlesticks. They show up right after the rapture, and they are the only light on the earth for the first half of the tribulation. I realize that most people say they show up at the second half, but I disagree, and I will show you why shortly. Now the Bible does not say who these men are, but it is certain that they are men and

48

not angels. Most people believe they are either Enoch and Elijah, or Moses and Elijah. Personally, I am convinced according to the transfiguration account in Matthew 17 that the two witnesses are Moses and Elijah. Whoever they are, they are filled with the power of God and are able to do great miracles. In verse 7, the beast kills them and leaves their bodies in the streets of Jerusalem, but not until they have finished their work for God. Verse 10 gives us some proof that nobody is yet saved on the earth, as it says "*all they that dwell upon the earth shall rejoice*" over the death of these two prophets of God. It said all didn't it? That means all on earth are glad that these guys are dead. Now that means nobody is saved yet, unless you think there are Christians on the moon!? In verse 11 the two candlesticks are brought back to life before the eyes of the whole world and ascend to heaven. In verse 13, I believe the one hundred forty-four thousand get saved as a direct result of the testimony of these two witnesses. Now, look closely at Revelation 11:14 *"The second woe is past; and, behold, the third woe cometh quickly."* Did you see what that said? This is more proof that one, the chapter is parenthetical, and two, these things we just read about from verses 1-13 are the first half of the tribulation, including the two witnesses. Do you see it? It said the second woe is past. Remember, the second woe is the sixth trumpet that sounded during the beginning of the second half of the tribulation period in Revelation 9:13.

So you see, these two witnesses show up in the first half of the tribulation, not the second half as most Bible teachers say. This chapter has been explaining some things about the first half of the tribulation in verses 1-14 which we know have already happened in Chapter 9, proving it is a review, a parenthetical chapter. Even parenthetical chapters have a sequence of order, as we note in the very next verses. Revelation 11:15-19 speaks of the seventh trumpet, the third woe. So the first fourteen verses explain the first half, and a bit past the middle, while verses 15-19 explain the second half of the tribulation. The seventh trumpet of verse 15 is actually explained in Revelation 15:1 with the seven vials.

LESSONS:
1. The tribulation is going to happen exactly as God planned.
2. God always leaves some light. These two prophets will be the only light left on the earth after the rapture for three and one-half years. The church is gone, all believers are gone, and the restraining power of the Holy Spirit over evil has been lifted. (2 Thessalonians 2:1-4)
3. The devil is no match for Spirit-filled Christians. The beast had no power over the two prophets until God let him.
4. The world rejoices when Christians fall.

PERSONAL APPLICATION:
1. Am I in the plan and will of God? (Romans 12:1-2)
2. Do I bring the light of Jesus to my small part of the world? (Matthew 5:16)
3. Am I filled with the Holy Spirit of God right now? (Ephesians 5:18)
4. When you fall, shock the world by getting back up. (Proverbs 24:16)

CLOSING: Compare Revelation 11:18 with Daniel 9:24 and see how they go together in showing the purpose of the Tribulation.

REVELATION Chapter 12

THEME: THREE WONDERS IN HEAVEN

SUMMARY:

We have gone through the seven seals, and have started the second half of the Tribulation in Chapters 8 and 9 with the blowing of six of the seven trumpets. Chapters 10 and 11 are parenthetical chapters. We saw that Chapter 11:1-14 discussed the first half of the Tribulation, giving us details about the two prophets who will be the only lights for God on the earth during the first half. They are killed by the beast and left in the streets of Jerusalem. God raises them from the dead and they ascend back to heaven, which leads to the one hundred forty-four thousand getting saved and fleeing for their lives. This all takes place right up to the second woe as we see in Revelation 11:14, which leaves no doubt as to the timeline of events.

This brings us to Revelation Chapter 12 which I call, "THREE WONDERS IN HEAVEN."

Revelation 12:1 "And there appeared a great wonder in heaven; a woman clothed with the sun, and the moon under her feet, and upon her head a crown of twelve stars:

2 And she being with child cried, travailing in birth, and pained to be delivered.

3 And there appeared another wonder in heaven; and behold a great red dragon, having seven heads and ten horns, and seven crowns upon his heads.

4 And his tail drew the third part of the stars of heaven, and did cast them to the earth: and the dragon stood before the woman which was ready to be delivered, for to devour her child as soon as it was born.

5 And she brought forth a man child, who was to rule all nations with a rod of iron: and her child was caught up unto God, and to his throne.

6 And the woman fled into the wilderness, where she hath a place prepared of God, that they should feed her there a thousand two hundred and threescore days.

7 And there was war in heaven: Michael and his angels fought against the dragon; and the dragon fought and his angels,

8 And prevailed not; neither was their place found any more in heaven.

9 And the great dragon was cast out, that old serpent, called the Devil, and Satan, which deceiveth the whole world: he was cast out into the earth, and his angels were cast out with him.

10 And I heard a loud voice saying in heaven, Now is come salvation, and strength, and the kingdom of our God, and the power of his Christ: for the accuser of our brethren is cast down, which accused them before our God day and night.

11 And they overcame him by the blood of the Lamb, and by the word of their testimony; and they loved not their lives unto the death.

12 Therefore rejoice, ye heavens, and ye that dwell in them. Woe to the inhabiters of the earth and of the sea! for the devil is come down unto you, having great wrath, because he knoweth that he hath but a short time.

13 And when the dragon saw that he was cast unto the earth, he persecuted the woman which brought forth the man child.

14 And to the woman were given two wings of a great eagle, that she might fly into the wilderness, into her place, where she is nourished for a time, and times, and half a time, from the face of the serpent.

15 And the serpent cast out of his mouth water as a flood after the woman, that he might cause her to be carried away of the flood.

16 And the earth helped the woman, and the earth opened her mouth, and swallowed up the flood which the dragon cast out of his mouth. 17 And the dragon was wroth with the woman, and went to make war with the remnant of her seed, which keep the commandments of God, and have the testimony of Jesus Christ."

This is an amazing chapter of Bible history and prophecy. This chapter covers at least six thousand years of history. Yes, you guessed it, it is another parenthetical chapter; therefore it is not in chronological order in the book. This chapter tells us where all this trouble began, and what shall be the end of it all. Verses 1-5 tell us about three wonders. I want you to see who they are:

1. Woman: Israel
2. Man Child: Jesus
3. Dragon: Satan

We see the woman had a crown of twelve stars symbolic of the twelve tribes. The child she is travailing to give birth to is the Messiah, the Lord Jesus Christ. The Dragon, the great red Dragon, is the devil. He is described in verse 4. We know Satan took a third of the angels in heaven with him when he rebelled against God. The devil has been trying to devour the Man Child since Genesis Chapter 3. He has been trying to keep Christ from coming into the world. We saw him try to kill the male children in Pharaoh's day, as well as in Herod's day when all the males two and under were killed in Bethlehem. Revelation 12:1-6 covers six thousand years of history, actually right up to the middle of the tribulation, as we see in verse 6.

In verses 7-13 we see that the devil is kicked out of heaven at the middle of the Tribulation. He will no longer be able to accuse us before God. He will realize that his time is short, and will pour out his wrath on Israel (Verse 13). This all takes place at the fifth trumpet as we noted in Revelation 9:1-12. (Notice the woe in verse 12, and compare with the three woes of Revelation 8:13 and 9:1.) In verses 14-17 we see the flight of Israel during the second half of the Tribulation, the time of Jacob's trouble, the time Jesus called the great tribulation in Matthew 24:15. Remember, Israel was at peace for the first half while the whole world was in turmoil. Now Israel is in great tribulation. Some have speculated that the eagle in verse 14 is the United States. It certainly could be, as we have always been a friend to them, but it is not clear if this is speaking of us or not. The earth is going to help Israel, some think Petra is the place that they will flee; this may be so. The earth also is going to swallow up the flood from the dragon's mouth and protect Israel while they flee. These one hundred forty-four thousand are the first people saved, and are going to be God's soul winners during the second half of the Tribulation (Revelation 14:1-4). Many will be martyred, but not before they witness for Christ.

LESSONS:

1. The nation of Israel is greatly loved by God. (Revelation 12:1)

2. Satan has always hated Israel because they were used to bring Christ into the world. (Revelation 12:13)

3. Satan hates God most of all, and persecutes God's people to get back at Him.

4. Satan has access to God and is the accuser of the brethren. (Revelation 12:10, Job 1 and 2)

5. Satan is kicked out of heaven at the middle of the seven years, and pours out his

wrath on Israel. (Revelation 12:7-13)

6. Satan is not in hell, but walks about as a roaring lion seeking to destroy.
   1 Peter 5:8, "*Be sober, be vigilant; because your adversary the devil, as a roaring lion, walketh about, seeking whom he may devour....*"

7. We overcome Satan in three ways according to Revelation 12:11 "*And they overcame him by the blood of the Lamb, and by the word of their testimony; and they loved not their lives unto the death.*"
   1. By the Blood of the Lamb ....Salvation
   2. By the word of our testimony ....Soul winning
   3. By loving not our lives ....Surrender and sacrifice

PERSONAL APPLICATION:

1. Have I given in to the world's prejudices against Israel? Remember, Satan hates them and wants us to hate them, too. Look what the Bible says concerning our relationship to Israel:
Genesis 12:3 "And I will bless them that bless thee, and curse him that curseth thee: and in thee shall all families of the earth be blessed.
Psalm 122:6 Pray for the peace of Jerusalem: they shall prosper that love thee."
2. Does Satan know of some sin in your life to report to God?
3. Would I consider myself a victorious Christian? Am I an "over comer?"

CLOSING: Never believe that you are any match for the devil without the Spirit of God upon you.

REVELATION Chapter 13

THEME: SATAN'S UNHOLY TRINITY

SUMMARY:

In Chapter 1, we saw the glory of Christ in the midst of the seven golden candlesticks. In Chapters 2 and 3 we saw seven letters written to seven literal churches, which are prophetic of the entire two thousand year church age. We saw the rapture of all believers in Chapter 4, and the seven sealed book in Chapter 5 that contains the judgments that will redeem Israel and the world. We know that the tribulation is from Chapter 6 through Chapter 19:11, and that it is seven years long. We know that this seven-year period is divided in two, three and one-half year periods. The first half is peaceful for Israel (Daniel 9:27), and the two prophets will be preaching in Jerusalem during this time, as we read in Chapter 11. These prophets will be killed as soon as Satan is cast to the earth at the middle of the tribulation as we read in Revelation 9:1 and Revelation 11:7-13, and he will break his treaty with Israel, defile the temple, and persecute the fleeing one hundred forty-four thousand that got saved after seeing the two prophets rise from the dead and ascend to heaven (Matthew 24:15-21).

Are you beginning to grasp the events of the tribulation now? Chapter 13 is parenthetical and shows us the devil's evil trinity.

Revelation 13:1 "And I stood upon the sand of the sea, and saw a beast rise up out of the sea, having seven heads and ten horns, and upon his horns ten crowns, and upon his heads the name of blasphemy.

2 And the beast which I saw was like unto a leopard, and his feet were as the feet of a bear, and his mouth as the mouth of a lion: and the dragon gave him his power, and his seat, and great authority.

3 And I saw one of his heads as it were wounded to death; and his deadly wound was healed: and all the world wondered after the beast.

4 And they worshipped the dragon which gave power unto the beast: and they worshipped the beast, saying, Who is like unto the beast? who is able to make war with him?

5 And there was given unto him a mouth speaking great things and blasphemies; and power was given unto him to continue forty and two months.

6 And he opened his mouth in blasphemy against God, to blaspheme his name, and his tabernacle, and them that dwell in heaven.

7 And it was given unto him to make war with the saints, and to overcome them: and power was given him over all kindreds, and tongues, and nations.

8 And all that dwell upon the earth shall worship him, whose names are not written in the book of life of the Lamb slain from the foundation of the world.

9 If any man have an ear, let him hear.

10 He that leadeth into captivity shall go into captivity: he that killeth with the sword must be killed with the sword. Here is the patience and the faith of the saints.

11 And I beheld another beast coming up out of the earth; and he had two horns like a lamb, and he spake as a dragon.

12 And he exerciseth all the power of the first beast before him, and causeth the earth and them which dwell therein to worship the first beast, whose deadly wound was healed.

13 And he doeth great wonders, so that he maketh fire come down from heaven on the earth in the sight of men,

14 And deceiveth them that dwell on the earth by the means of those miracles which he had power to do in the sight of the beast; saying to them that dwell on the earth, that they should make an image to the beast, which had the wound by a sword, and did live.

15 And he had power to give life unto the image of the beast, that the image of the beast should both speak, and cause that as many as would not worship the image of the beast should be killed.

16 And he causeth all, both small and great, rich and poor, free and bond, to receive a mark in their right hand, or in their foreheads:

17 And that no man might buy or sell, save he that had the mark, or the name of the beast, or the number of his name.

18 Here is wisdom. Let him that hath understanding count the number of the beast: for it is the number of a man; and his number is Six hundred threescore and six."

The devil is a deceiver; he has a counterfeit to everything God has. He has a counterfeit Bible, a counterfeit to the Holy Spirit, a counterfeit Christ, counterfeit gifts, and on and on we could go. Chapter 13 deals with the unholy trinity. Just as God is triune, Satan has his version of the trinity:

FATHER	SON	HOLY SPIRIT
=	=	=
SATAN	ANTICHRIST	FALSE PROPHET

Satan represents God the Father. The Antichrist represents God the Son, Jesus. Antichrist is a false christ. Some people believe the Antichrist is Judas reincarnated. Regardless, he will be an imitator of Christ, and will direct people to worship Satan. He arises out of the sea in Revelation 13:1 (which actually takes place in Revelation 6:1-2) with the opening of the first seal. This is symbolic of his political world leadership, (or should we say dictatorship?). Antichrist gets his power from Satan as we see in verses 2 and 4. In Revelation 13:5-6 we see that his most evil reign begins when he enters and defiles the temple at the middle of the tribulation, which corresponds with Revelation 9, Matthew 24:15-21, and 2 Thessalonians 2:4. When Satan is cast out of heaven, it becomes hell on earth! Notice that all the unbelievers that dwell on the earth will worship him.

The false prophet, which is the second beast that comes out of the land in Revelation 13:11, will be the religious leader during the tribulation. See another reference to him in Revelation 16:13: *"And I saw three unclean spirits like frogs come out of the mouth of the dragon, and out of the mouth of the beast, and out of the mouth of the false prophet."*

Just as the Holy Spirit points men to Jesus, the false prophet will point men to the Antichrist during the tribulation. He will head up the one-world apostate church, also called religious Babylon that falls in Revelation 17. He will do great wonders and deceive many on the earth into worshiping the Antichrist. He will lead the people to worship an image of the beast which he will cause to talk. This could be some sort of video, and whoever will not worship this image will be killed. This false prophet will be the one to lead the world into receiving the mark of the beast that will be needed to buy or sell (Revelation 13:15). This mark of the beast will start during the second half, after the Antichrist enters the temple and declares he is God and the false prophet leads people to worship him. We see that this mark of the beast is the number 666 in verse 18.

The false prophet will be a pawn used by the Antichrist to control the world. The Antichrist shows his gratitude by overthrowing him in Revelation 17:16, which is no surprise to those of us who know the wiles of Satan!

LESSONS:
1. The devil is a master of deception.
2 Corinthians 11:14: "And no marvel; for Satan himself is transformed into an angel of light.
2. It is dangerous to trust feelings and emotions. Live by faith, not by feelings!
Jeremiah 17:9: "The heart is deceitful above all things, and desperately wicked: who can know it?"
3. Miracles, or unexplained happenings, are not necessarily evidence of the Spirit of God. (Revelation 13:2-15)

PERSONAL APPLICATION:
1. Always "try" the spirits to see if they be of God. *1John 4:1: "Beloved, believe not every spirit, but try the spirits whether they are of God: because many false prophets are gone out into the world."*
2. Am I allowing the Holy Spirit to use me to point others to Jesus?
3. Is my life governed by feelings or by the Bible?

CLOSING:
Daniel 2, Daniel 7, and Revelation 13:1-2 are all basically the same story. They speak of four world kingdoms that rule the whole world. Actually, there are five if you count the revived Roman Empire of the tribulation. There have only been four times in human history that the world has been under one leader. The fifth time will be during the tribulation, and will be the revived Roman Empire, a renewal of the fourth empire made up of the ten European nations. These are all in place at the present time I am writing, and even have a common currency, the Euro dollar. Antichrist will head up this empire. In the chart, I give the empire, it's ruler, and how they are described in the Bible. Notice that Nebuchadnezzar saw them as metals in the form of a statue. That is how worldly man thinks, isn't it? Man thinks in terms of value and wealth. However, the vision that Daniel saw in Daniel 7 tells of the same world empires, but God describes them as wild beasts. God is saying that they are untamed wild beasts that devour and destroy. Notice that Revelation 13 shows that the kingdom of the antichrist will have qualities from each of the four kingdoms of the past.

World Kingdoms	Daniel Chapter 2	Daniel Chapter 7	Revelation 13
1. Babylon Daniel's day 605 B.C. Nebuchadnezzar	Head of gold	Lion with eagles wings	Mouth of lion
2. Media-Persia Alexander the Great!	Chest and arms of silver	Bear	Feet of bear
3. Greece	Belly and thigh of brass	Leopard	Like leopard
4. Rome	Feet of iron	Dreadful beast	A beast
5. Antichrist	Feet of iron and clay (ten toes)	Ten horns	Ten horns
6. Christ's Kingdom	Stone cut out without hands (Daniel 2:34)	Everlasting Kingdom (Daniel 7:27)	

NOTE: John records them backwards in Revelation 13 because he is looking from future to the past. Read and study Daniel 2 and 7 and realize we are very close to the end.

REVELATION Chapter 14

THEME: ONE HUNDRED FORTY-FOUR THOUSAND WITH THE EVERLASTING GOSPEL

SUMMARY:

Chapters 6-19 describe the seven year tribulation. This period is divided in two, three and one-half year periods. The second half, called the great tribulation, begins in Chapter 8 with the seven trumpets. Remember, the judgments are a series of sevens: seven seals, seven trumpets, and seven vials. Satan was cast out of heaven in the fifth trumpet in Chapter 9. Chapters 10-14 are all parenthetical in nature, and give us some more detailed information to help us understand the events.

Now let's look at Chapter 14:

Revelation 14: "And I looked, and, lo, a Lamb stood on the mount Sion, and with him an hundred forty and four thousand, having his Father's name written in their foreheads. 2 And I heard a voice from heaven, as the voice of many waters, and as the voice of a great thunder: and I heard the voice of harpers harping with their harps: 3 And they sung as it were a new song before the throne, and before the four beasts, and the elders: and no man could learn that song but the hundred and forty and four thousand, which were redeemed from the earth. 4 These are they which were not defiled with women; for they are virgins. These are they which follow the Lamb whithersoever he goeth. These were redeemed from among men, being the firstfruits unto God and to the Lamb. 5 And in their mouth was found no guile: for they are without fault before the throne of God. 6 And I saw another angel fly in the midst of heaven, having the everlasting gospel to preach unto them that dwell on the earth, and to every nation, and kindred, and tongue, and people, 7 Saying with a loud voice, Fear God, and give glory to him; for the hour of his judgment is come: and worship him that made heaven, and earth, and the sea, and the fountains of waters. 8 And there followed another angel, saying, Babylon is fallen, is fallen, that great city, because she made all nations drink of the wine of the wrath of her fornication. 9 And the third angel followed them, saying with a loud voice, If any man worship the beast and his image, and receive his mark in his forehead, or in his hand, 10 The same shall drink of the wine of the wrath of God, which is poured out without mixture into the cup of his indignation; and he shall be tormented with fire and brimstone in the presence of the holy angels, and in the presence of the Lamb: 11 And the smoke of their torment ascendeth up for ever and ever: and they have no rest day nor night, who worship the beast and his image, and whosoever receiveth the mark of his name. 12 Here is the patience of the saints: here are they that keep the commandments of God, and the faith of Jesus. 13 And I heard a voice from heaven saying unto me, Write, Blessed are the dead which die in the Lord from henceforth: Yea, saith the Spirit, that they may rest from their labours; and their works do follow them. 14 And I looked, and behold a white cloud, and upon the cloud one sat like unto the Son of man, having on his head a golden crown, and in his hand a sharp sickle. 15 And another angel came out of the temple, crying with a loud voice to him that sat on the cloud, Thrust in thy sickle, and reap: for the time is come for thee to reap; for the harvest of the earth is ripe. 16 And he that sat on the cloud thrust in his sickle on the earth; and the earth was reaped 17 And another angel came out of the temple which is in heaven, he also having a sharp sickle. 18 And another angel came out from the altar, which had power over fire; and cried with a loud cry to him that had the sharp sickle, saying, Thrust in thy sharp sickle, and gather the clusters of the vine of the earth; for her grapes are fully ripe 19 And the angel thrust in his sickle into the earth, and gathered the vine of the earth, and cast it into the great winepress of the wrath of God. 20 And the winepress was trodden without the city, and blood came out of the winepress, even unto the horse bridles, by the space of a thousand and six hundred furlongs."

The theme of this parenthetical chapter is the work of the one hundred forty-four thousand with the everlasting gospel. It is obvious that it is parenthetical because it follows no time line, but it also covers the second coming of Christ at the end of the tribulation (Revelation 14:13-20).

We see in verse 3 the one hundred forty-four thousand were redeemed from the earth. This happens at the middle of the tribulation after the fifth trumpet in Chapter 9. I believe that Revelation 11:13 is a reference to their salvation. Verse 4 is symbolic of the pure and separated lives of these new converts. Notice also that they are the "firstfruits," the first people saved during the tribulation. In verse 5 we see that all believers are washed clean by the blood of the Lamb. In verses 6 and 7 these new converts are given the power of God to preach the gospel. Verse 8 jumps ahead to show the fall of Babylon spoken of in Revelation 17 and 18. Verses 9-11 give a warning concerning the worship of the beast and taking his mark. Revelation 14:12-13 speaks of blessings to the saved. Revelation 14:14 relates to the second coming of Christ at the battle of Armageddon (Revelation 19:11), and Revelation 14:15-20 is the final harvest of the earth that takes place right before the redeemed return with Christ.

LESSONS:

1. The one hundred forty-four thousand Jews are the first people saved during the tribulation. (Revelation 14:4)

2. God's people have a song that the lost world cannot sing. (Revelation 14:3)

3. The Bible speaks of two resurrections. 1 Corinthians 15:22-23: *"For as in Adam all die, even so in Christ shall all be made alive. But every man in his own order: Christ the firstfruits; afterward they that are Christ's at his coming."*
Revelation 20:6: *"Blessed and holy is he that hath part in the first resurrection: on such the second death hath no power, but they shall be priests of God and of Christ, and shall reign with him a thousand years."*

This is speaking of bodily resurrections. When a saved person died before the crucifixion of Christ, his body went in the ground, and his *spirit* went to Abraham's bosom as seen in Luke 16:19-31. This is the place called "Paradise" that Christ promised to the thief on the cross in Luke 23:43, which is so misunderstood by many. When Christ paid the penalty for sin, He became the first to rise bodily from the dead. He lead the souls in Paradise to heaven, which is where all the saved who die after the cross go at death (Ephesians 4:8-10). However, we will not have our resurrected *bodies* yet. At the rapture, all the bodies of the saved, both alive and dead, will be resurrected. This is the main harvest. I Thessalonians 4:15-17: *"For this we say unto you by the word of the Lord, that we which are alive and remain unto the coming of the Lord shall not prevent them which are asleep. For the Lord himself shall descend from heaven with a shout, with the voice of the archangel, and with the trump of God: and the dead in Christ shall rise first: Then we which are alive and remain shall be caught up together with them in the clouds, to meet the Lord in the air: and so shall we ever be with the Lord."*

RESURRECTION OF THE SAVED	RESURRECTION OF THE LOST
In three stages:	(Great White Throne Judgment)
	Rev 20:4-5 at end of one
	thousand years

1. Firstfruits: Calvary- Matthew 27:50-53
                               1 Corinthians 15:17-26
2. Main harvest: Rapture- Revelation 4,
                               I Thessalonians 4:16, Corinthians 15:51-52
3. Gleanings: Second coming-Revelation 14:14-17

Note: You can liken this unto the three stages of harvesting a crop.

PERSONAL APPLICATION:

1. Do you have the song of the Lord in your heart?
2. Are you 100% sure you're redeemed and on your way to heaven for a Bible reason?
3. It is clear from Revelation 14:9 that receiving the mark of the beast comes to those who worship the beast, and not just by holding out one's hand and getting a tattoo or mark. Also true, salvation does not come just by acknowledging the facts of the gospel, but by acting upon and putting our faith and trust in the payment for our sins that Jesus Christ has paid! Many folks know the facts about the gospel, but have not acted upon those facts by placing their faith in Christ.

CLOSING: Friend, have you made certain your eternal destiny?

REVELATION Chapter 15

THEME: SEVEN LAST PLAGUES REVEALED

Revelation 15:1-8: "And I saw another sign in heaven, great and marvellous, seven angels having the seven last plagues; for in them is filled up the wrath of God. And I saw as it were a sea of glass mingled with fire: and them that had gotten the victory over the beast, and over his image, and over his mark, and over the number of his name, stand on the sea of glass, having the harps of God. And they sing the song of Moses the servant of God, and the song of the Lamb, saying, Great and marvellous are thy works, Lord God Almighty; just and true are thy ways, thou King of saints. Who shall not fear thee, O Lord, and glorify thy name? for thou only art holy: for all nations shall come and worship before thee; for thy judgments are made manifest. And after that I looked, and, behold, the temple of the tabernacle of the testimony in heaven was opened: And the seven angels came out of the temple, having the seven plagues, clothed in pure and white linen, and having their breasts girded with golden girdles. And one of the four beasts gave unto the seven angels seven golden vials full of the wrath of God, who liveth for ever and ever. And the temple was filled with smoke from the glory of God, and from his power; and no man was able to enter into the temple, until the seven plagues of the seven angels were fulfilled."

SUMMARY: We just finished a parenthetical series of chapters from Chapter 10-Chapter 14. When we read Revelation 15:1 it is obvious we are going back to the place we left off in the tribulation, which was the seventh trumpet, the third and last woe, which was revealed in Revelation 11:14-15. Remember, Chapter 11 is parenthetical through verse 14, but it does reveal the seventh trumpet in Revelation 11:15-19. Notice how Revelation 11:19 leads right into Revelation 15:5. Revelation 11:19: *"And the temple of God was opened in heaven, and there was seen in his temple the ark of his testament: and there were lightnings, and voices, and thunderings, and an earthquake, and great hail."* Compare that with Revelation 15:5: *"And after that I looked, and, behold, the temple of the tabernacle of the testimony in heaven was opened...."*

Let me explain: Revelation Chapter 6 begins the tribulation with the opening of the first six seals. Chapter 7 is parenthetical and is inserted to explain about the one hundred forty-four thousand who will be saved at the middle of the tribulation. You could actually read Chapters 6 and 8, skipping Chapter 7, and not miss a thing. Chapter 8 and 9 are the events that take place at the beginning of the second half and end at the sixth trumpet which is also the second woe. Chapter 10 is inserted to show what prophecy should do to our stomach. Revelation 11:1-13 is also parenthetical. It goes back and explains that there are two witnesses in Jerusalem right after the rapture who will be God's candlesticks, the only light on the earth. The chapter shows that they will be killed by the Antichrist, and then the one hundred forty-four thousand will get saved (Revelation 11:13). When we get to Revelation 11:14, we see the timeline for the death of these two witnesses, as well as the conversion for the one hundred forty-four thousand Jews which takes place right after the second woe. This is also the sounding of the fifth trumpet which we saw in Revelation 8:13-9:12. Now Revelation 11:15 brings us back to the place we left off in Chapter 9, and shows us the seventh

60

trumpet sounding. The seventh trumpet reveals the seven last plagues of the tribulation, the seven vial judgments. They take place in Chapter 16. Before we get to them, Revelation Chapter 12 is added to explain the three wonders, so we will know why the devil hates Israel and why and when he will turn his attack on them during the second half of the tribulation. Chapter 13 is inserted to explain Satan's trinity, and show the rise and power of the Antichrist and the false prophet. Chapter 14 is inserted to explain what the one hundred forty-four thousand will be doing after they get saved. When we get to Chapter 15, we are back to where we left off in Revelation 11:15-19 and the seven vial judgments. Chapter 15 is actually an introduction to Chapter 16 with the pouring out of those seven vials, and is the shortest chapter in Revelation. Once we get through the seven vials, chapters 17 and 18 shows the fall of religious and political Babylon, which takes place near the end. Then Chapter 19 shows the battle of Armageddon and the second coming of Christ which ends the tribulation and ushers in the Millennium. Are you still with me? <u>What I am saying is that the chronological timeline of the tribulation is as follows: Revelation Chapter 6, Chapter 8, Chapter 9, Chapter 11:15-19, Chapter 15, Chapter 16, Chapter 19:1-11. The other chapters are important, but not in chronological order. They are added to explain some things, they are parenthetical.</u>

Now let's look at some lessons from this brief chapter, Revelation 15.

LESSONS:

1. These seven last plagues are the wrath of God. (Revelation 15:1)

The seven seals are basically wars and turmoil caused by man. The seven trumpets are the results of Satan's wrath upon man. These seven vials are the wrath of God upon earth.

2. Glass mingled with fire symbolizes judgment. (Revelation 15:2)

3. We can have victory through Christ, no matter how bad things get. (Revelation 15:2)

4. See how Revelation 11:19 flows right into Revelation 15:5 in the timeline?

5. Many believe Revelation 15:8 means nobody else gets saved after this point.

PERSONAL APPLICATION:

1. If I am not saved, I, too, am under the condemnation and wrath of God!

Romans 8:1: "There is therefore now no condemnation to them which are in Christ Jesus, who walk not after the flesh, but after the Spirit."
John 5:24: "Verily, verily, I say unto you, He that heareth my word, and believeth on him that sent me, hath everlasting life, and shall not come into condemnation; but is passed from death unto life."
John 3:18: "He that believeth on him is not condemned: but he that believeth not is condemned already, because he hath not believed in the name of the only begotten Son of God."
John 3:36: "He that believeth on the Son hath everlasting life: and he that believeth not the Son shall not see life; but the wrath of God abideth on him."

2. Will I have any rewards in heaven?

Believers will not be judged for their sin, because our sins are under the blood of

Christ; however, we will stand at the judgment seat of Christ and be judged according to the good we have done.

1 Corinthians 3:13-15: "Every man's work shall be made manifest: for the day shall declare it, because it shall be revealed by fire; and the fire shall try every man's work of what sort it is. If any man's work abide which he hath built thereupon, he shall receive a reward. If any man's work shall be burned, he shall suffer loss: but he himself shall be saved; yet so as by fire."

3. Am I living a victorious life?

It is tragic that we who have it so easy, have so little victory in our lives. In many ways, persecution becomes a blessing to God's people.

CLOSING: The next chapter will go into detail as the seven vials are poured out.

REVELATION Chapter 16

THEME: THE SEVEN VIALS OF GOD'S WRATH

SUMMARY:

In Chapter 1, we saw Christ in the midst of His church. In Chapters 2 and 3 we saw the seven letters written to the seven churches, and we clearly see that these seven churches have a prophetic meaning. They represent seven ages of church history. We are now living in the last age. In Chapter 4, the rapture took place and we saw all believers taken to heaven. Chapter 5 showed us the seven sealed book that Christ opened which began the tribulation on earth that lasts seven years. We saw the four horsemen ride and one-fourth of the world's population die. A billion people could die and go to hell in these first four seals alone! We saw in Chapter 7 that there are one hundred forty-four thousand Jews going to be saved, but not until the middle of the tribulation. In the meantime, the two witnesses of Chapter 11 are preaching to Jerusalem during the first half of the tribulation. Chapter 8 shows us a pause in heaven for half an hour, possibly "half-time." No doubt, Chapter 9 is the "Great Tribulation" of Matthew 24:21, the time called "Jacob's Trouble." It is the "midst of the week" of Daniel 9:27 where Satan is cast out of heaven and enters and defiles the Jewish temple in Jerusalem and breaks his treaty with Israel. We saw this in Revelation 12, Daniel 9:27, and Matthew 24:15. The Antichrist at this time kills the two witnesses and leaves their dead bodies in the streets. But three and one-half days later, God resurrects them and they ascend to heaven, which leads to the conversion of the one hundred forty-four thousand Jews who then flee for their lives. They become the preachers during the second half and lead many to Christ. The seventh trumpet ushers in the seven vial judgments that were introduced to us in Chapter 15 which we just looked at. These seven vials are the wrath of Almighty God! Chapter 16 goes into great detail concerning the pouring out of these vials, or bowls. As we look at them, remember that this is near the very end of the tribulation and comes upon the earth very rapidly.

Revelation 16:1: "And I heard a great voice out of the temple saying to the seven angels, Go your ways, and pour out the vials of the wrath of God upon the earth. 2 And the first went, and poured out his vial upon the earth; and there fell a noisome and grievous sore upon the men which had the mark of the beast, and upon them which worshipped his image. 3 And the second angel poured out his vial upon the sea; and it became as the blood of a dead man: and every living soul died in the sea. 4 And the third angel poured out his vial upon the rivers and fountains of waters; and they became blood. 5 And I heard the angel of the waters say, Thou art righteous, O Lord, which art, and wast, and shalt be, because thou hast judged thus. 6 For they have shed the blood of saints and prophets, and thou hast given them blood to drink; for they are worthy. 7 And I heard another out of the altar say, Even so, Lord God Almighty, true and righteous are thy judgments. 8 And the fourth angel poured out his vial upon the sun; and power was given unto him to scorch men with fire. 9 And men were scorched with great heat, and blasphemed the name of God, which hath power over these plagues: and they repented not to give him glory. 10 And the fifth angel poured out his vial upon the seat of the beast; and his kingdom was full of darkness; and they gnawed their tongues for pain, 11 And blasphemed the God of heaven because of their pains and their sores, and repented not of their deeds. 12 And the sixth angel poured out his vial upon the great river

Euphrates; and the water thereof was dried up, that the way of the kings of the east might be prepared. 13 And I saw three unclean spirits like frogs come out of the mouth of the dragon, and out of the mouth of the beast, and out of the mouth of the false prophet. 14 For they are the spirits of devils, working miracles, which go forth unto the kings of the earth and of the whole world, to gather them to the battle of that great day of God Almighty. 15 Behold, I come as a thief. Blessed is he that watcheth, and keepeth his garments, lest he walk naked, and they see his shame. 16 And he gathered them together into a place called in the Hebrew tongue Armageddon. 17 And the seventh angel poured out his vial into the air; and there came a great voice out of the temple of heaven, from the throne, saying, It is done. 18 And there were voices, and thunders, and lightnings; and there was a great earthquake, such as was not since men were upon the earth, so mighty an earthquake, and so great. 19 And the great city was divided into three parts, and the cities of the nations fell: and great Babylon came in remembrance before God, to give unto her the cup of the wine of the fierceness of his wrath. 20 And every island fled away, and the mountains were not found. 21 And there fell upon men a great hail out of heaven, every stone about the weight of a talent: and men blasphemed God because of the plague of the hail; for the plague thereof was exceeding great."

As I said before, the seven seals are mostly man fighting against man. At the halfway point of the tribulation, the turmoil on the earth seems to be caused by Satan. He is cast to the earth and takes out his wrath against Israel, the woman that "brought forth the man child" of Revelation 12. Now we have come to the last set of seven judgments, the seven vials. This takes place near the end of the tribulation, and is more severe than anything we have seen yet. It is the vengeance and wrath of God upon a sin-cursed earth!

LESSONS:

1. Take each vial literally unless context shows it is symbolic.
   (For instance, verse 3 says the sea became AS blood, showing symbolism.)

2. These vials are the judgments of God.

3. These judgments are against the lost people on the earth. No harm will come to those recently saved people. Revelation 16:2

4. God is righteous and just even in His wrath. Revelation 16:5-7

5. God brings vengeance upon those who persecute His servants. Revelation 16:6

6. The sixth vial prepares the way for China's two hundred million man army to march toward Israel for the final battle, the battle of Armageddon. Revelation 16:12-16

7. The fall of Babylon in Revelation 16:19 is actually explained in great detail in Revelation Chapters 17 and 18. For the timeline, you could actually go from Chapter 16 to Chapter 19. Chapters 17 and 18 are there to show the judgment of Babylon near the end of the seven-year tribulation.

PERSONAL APPLICATION:

1. Pray for and witness to your lost loved ones, lest they fall under the wrath of God.

2. Have you ever found yourself bitter and angry about something God allowed to happen in your life? Take a moment and read Revelation 16:5-7 and confess that God is holy and just.
3. Remember that "vengeance is mine, sayeth the Lord."
4. Is the church I attend part of the one-world religious system that God loathes? Revelation 16:19

CLOSING: We are now at the final moments of the tribulation. Christ is about to return in glory in Revelation 19:6, but first, we are given a look at the fall of the one-world church and one-world government headed by Antichrist. We shall see this in Revelation 17 and 18.

REVELATION Chapter 17

THEME: FALL OF RELIGIOUS BABYLON

Revelation 17:1: And there came one of the seven angels which had the seven vials, and talked with me, saying unto me, Come hither; I will shew unto thee the judgment of the great whore that sitteth upon many waters: 2 With whom the kings of the earth have committed fornication, and the inhabitants of the earth have been made drunk with the wine of her fornication. 3 So he carried me away in the spirit into the wilderness: and I saw a woman sit upon a scarlet coloured beast, full of names of blasphemy, having seven heads and ten horns. 4 And the woman was arrayed in purple and scarlet colour, and decked with gold and precious stones and pearls, having a golden cup in her hand full of abominations and filthiness of her fornication: 5 And upon her forehead was a name written, MYSTERY, BABYLON THE GREAT, THE MOTHER OF HARLOTS AND ABOMINATIONS OF THE EARTH. 6 And I saw the woman drunken with the blood of the saints, and with the blood of the martyrs of Jesus: and when I saw her, I wondered with great admiration. 7 And the angel said unto me, Wherefore didst thou marvel? I will tell thee the mystery of the woman, and of the beast that carrieth her, which hath the seven heads and ten horns. 8 The beast that thou sawest was, and is not; and shall ascend out of the bottomless pit, and go into perdition: and they that dwell on the earth shall wonder, whose names were not written in the book of life from the foundation of the world, when they behold the beast that was, and is not, and yet is. 9 And here is the mind which hath wisdom. The seven heads are seven mountains, on which the woman sitteth. 10 And there are seven kings: five are fallen, and one is, and the other is not yet come; and when he cometh, he must continue a short space. 11 And the beast that was, and is not, even he is the eighth, and is of the seven, and goeth into perdition. 12 And the ten horns which thou sawest are ten kings, which have received no kingdom as yet; but receive power as kings one hour with the beast. 13 These have one mind, and shall give their power and strength unto the beast. 14 These shall make war with the Lamb, and the Lamb shall overcome them: for he is Lord of lords, and King of kings: and they that are with him are called, and chosen, and faithful. 15 And he saith unto me, The waters which thou sawest, where the whore sitteth, are peoples, and multitudes, and nations, and tongues. 16 And the ten horns which thou sawest upon the beast, these shall hate the whore, and shall make her desolate and naked, and shall eat her flesh, and burn her with fire. 17 For God hath put in their hearts to fulfil his will, and to agree, and give their kingdom unto the beast, until the words of God shall be fulfilled. 18 And the woman which thou sawest is that great city, which reigneth over the kings of the earth."

SUMMARY:

Chapter 17 is a pause at the end of the tribulation to show us the fall of the one-world religious system. This will take place during the pouring out of the last plagues of the earth, the seven vial judgments of Chapter 16. I believe the one-world church is already in place and is only awaiting the removal of the Holy Spirit and born again right wing fanatical believers from the earth in the rapture. (Did you happen to watch the national prayer meeting that took place after the 9/11 attacks?) I also believe that it is most likely the Catholic church that will head up the one-world church. Let me give you some reasons why many believe, as I do, that this religious Babylon is the Catholic Church.

1. In verses 1 and 2 we see that "the great whore" is yoked with kings and nations. She is yoked with politics. History shows that since 313 A.D. the Catholic Church became the state religion. By the way, even today the Vatican is considered a state, and has ambassadors in nearly every country, including America. Did you know that America has an ambassador to the Vatican? Some people say that the Catholic Church owns more property in America than any other, including our own government. By the way, Constantine was the man who merged the state with the Catholic Church in

66

313 A.D. He also brought the pagan doctrines of: worshiping Mary as the queen of heaven, purgatory, holy water, candles, a celibate priesthood, and many other pagan beliefs into the Catholic church. Did you know that the Catholic Church helped Hitler rise to power? This was made public and the Pope apologized for this just a short time ago. I said earlier, Satan always has a man who is his antichrist, and the Pope would most likely have been his false prophet had God's timing been right. (II Thessalonians 2:7)

2. We see the roots of the Catholic beliefs way back in Genesis 10 and 11 in the story of Nimrod and the tower of Babel, which is Babylon. You see, Babel, or Babylon, was more than a city. It was a symbol of a political system of government that has never died, but is still at the root of this world's system today.

3. Rome is the only city that fits the description of Revelation 17:18.

4. Rome is known as the city of the seven hills. Revelation 17:9

5. Revelation 17:4 speaks of the woman being clothed with purple and scarlet. These are the very colors of the bishops and cardinals today.

6. In Revelation 17:3 we see that this woman sits upon the beast which is symbolic of religion and politics mixed together. In 313 A.D. the Catholic Church merged with the state under Constantine. The Catholic Church is very political even today.

7. In Revelation 17:4 we see that this religious system is very wealthy. There is no doubt, the Catholic Church is worth billions of dollars. The Vatican alone is priceless. I walked through it back in the early 80's and saw the golden tapestries. There is not any other religious system on the earth that comes close to the wealth of the Catholic Church.

8. Maybe the greatest proof of all is Revelation 17:6 where we see that this great whore is drunken with the blood of God's people. It is a historical fact that the Catholic Church is responsible for the slaughter of countless Christians.

LESSONS:

1. Judgment day is soon coming for the great whore. (Revelation 17:1)

2. Politicians court this great whore because of her wealth, power, and influence. (Revelation 17:2)

3. This world's religion looks good on the outside, but it is filthy on the inside. (Revelation 17:4)

4. God makes it clear in bold print that the great whore is the mother of all false religion and wickedness in the earth. She spawns them. (Revelation 17:5)

5. The beast shall destroy the one-world religious system once he has used it to achieve his objectives. (Revelation 17:16-17)

PERSONAL APPLICATION:

1. Remember to love the sinner while hating the false religious system.

2. Are you in the public arena to some extent, and do you compromise your beliefs to earn the favor of the rich and powerful? (There are very few politicians that you can trust.)

3. Are you on the inside what you show to others on the outside?

4. Is your life influencing people for bad or for good?

5. When the world gets all it can from you, it casts you aside.

CLOSING: Notice John's reaction to this one-world church of the tribulation in Revelation 17:6. Could it be that he is startled by how something that is called a church could deceive the world into thinking it is something good?

REVELATION Chapter 18

THEME: FALL OF POLITICAL BABYLON

SUMMARY:

In Chapter 17 we saw the fall of religious Babylon, the one-world church headed up by the beast from the land (Revelation 13:11-18), who is the false prophet, the third person of the unholy trinity. Chapter 18 continues with the pause at the end of the vial judgments to show us the fall of commercial or political Babylon. This is the fall of the one-world government system that the Antichrist heads up as he is given power to do so in the first seal in Revelation 6:2. He is the rider on the white horse, the beast from the sea in Revelation 13:1-10.

Revelation 18:1: "And after these things I saw another angel come down from heaven, having great power; and the earth was lightened with his glory. 2 And he cried mightily with a strong voice, saying, Babylon the great is fallen, is fallen, and is become the habitation of devils, and the hold of every foul spirit, and a cage of every unclean and hateful bird. 3 For all nations have drunk of the wine of the wrath of her fornication, and the kings of the earth have committed fornication with her, and the merchants of the earth are waxed rich through the abundance of her delicacies. 4 And I heard another voice from heaven, saying, Come out of her, my people, that ye be not partakers of her sins, and that ye receive not of her plagues. 5 For her sins have reached unto heaven, and God hath remembered her iniquities. 6 Reward her even as she rewarded you, and double unto her double according to her works: in the cup which she hath filled fill to her double. 7 How much she hath glorified herself, and lived deliciously, so much torment and sorrow give her: for she saith in her heart, I sit a queen, and am no widow, and shall see no sorrow. 8 Therefore shall her plagues come in one day, death, and mourning, and famine; and she shall be utterly burned with fire: for strong is the Lord God who judgeth her. 9 And the kings of the earth, who have committed fornication and lived deliciously with her, shall bewail her, and lament for her, when they shall see the smoke of her burning, 10 Standing afar off for the fear of her torment, saying, Alas, alas, that great city Babylon, that mighty city! for in one hour is thy judgment come. 11 And the merchants of the earth shall weep and mourn over her; for no man buyeth their merchandise any more: 12 The merchandise of gold, and silver, and precious stones, and of pearls, and fine linen, and purple, and silk, and scarlet, and all thyine wood, and all manner vessels of ivory, and all manner vessels of most precious wood, and of brass, and iron, and marble, 13 And cinnamon, and odours, and ointments, and frankincense, and wine, and oil, and fine flour, and wheat, and beasts, and sheep, and horses, and chariots, and slaves, and souls of men. 14 And the fruits that thy soul lusted after are departed from thee, and all things which were dainty and goodly are departed from thee, and thou shalt find them no more at all. 15 The merchants of these things, which were made rich by her, shall stand afar off for the fear of her torment, weeping and wailing, 16 And saying, Alas, alas, that great city, that was clothed in fine linen, and purple, and scarlet, and decked with gold, and precious stones, and pearls! 17 For in one hour so great riches is come to nought. And every shipmaster, and all the company in ships, and sailors, and as many as trade by sea, stood afar off, 18 And cried when they saw the smoke of her burning, saying, What city is like unto this great city! 19 And they cast dust on their heads, and cried, weeping and wailing, saying, Alas, alas, that great city, wherein were made rich all that had ships in the sea by reason of her costliness! for in one hour is she made desolate. 20 Rejoice over her, thou heaven, and ye holy apostles and prophets; for God hath avenged you on her. 21 And a mighty angel took up a stone like a great millstone, and cast it into the sea, saying, Thus with violence shall that great city Babylon be thrown down, and shall be found no more at all. 22 And the voice of harpers, and musicians, and of pipers, and trumpeters, shall be heard no more at all in thee; and no craftsman, of whatsoever craft he be, shall be found any more in thee; and the sound of a millstone shall be heard no more at all in thee; 23 And the light of a candle shall shine no more at all in thee; and the voice of the bridegroom and of the bride shall be heard no more at all in thee: for thy merchants were the great men of the earth; for by thy sorceries were all nations deceived. 24 And in her was found the blood of prophets, and of saints, and of all that were slain upon the earth."

LESSONS:
1. The one-world system will not last long. (Revelation 18:1-2)

2. All the nations of the world will be a part of this system, which is the revived Roman Empire.

3. God's people are not to be a part of the wicked and Godless world's system. (Revelation 18:4)

4. Nothing done down here on earth goes unnoticed by God. (Revelation 18:5)

5. The one-world system will completely crash in one day. (Revelation 18:8-10)

6. The businessmen of the world will weep and wail at the loss of their fortune, making the crash of 1929 pale in comparison. (Revelation 18:9-19)

7. Vengeance is the Lord's, and it will come. (Revelation 18:20-24)

PERSONAL APPLICATION:
1. Am I trusting in the Lord or the world's system to care for me?
2. Do I live day to day realizing that God is watching me?
3. Is your treasure in stocks and bonds, or in heaven?
4. Do I often seek revenge on those who wrong me?

CLOSING: With the ending of Chapters 17 and 18, we now come to Chapter 19 and the end of the tribulation as Christ comes in the clouds with His saints.

REVELATION Chapter 19

THEME: SECOND COMING OF CHRIST AT ARMAGEDDON

Revelation 19:1: "And after these things I heard a great voice of much people in heaven, saying, Alleluia; Salvation, and glory, and honour, and power, unto the Lord our God: 2 For true and righteous are his judgments: for he hath judged the great whore, which did corrupt the earth with her fornication, and hath avenged the blood of his servants at her hand. 3 And again they said, Alleluia. And her smoke rose up for ever and ever. 4 And the four and twenty elders and the four beasts fell down and worshipped God that sat on the throne, saying, Amen; Alleluia. 5 And a voice came out of the throne, saying, Praise our God, all ye his servants, and ye that fear him, both small and great. 6 And I heard as it were the voice of a great multitude, and as the voice of many waters, and as the voice of mighty thunderings, saying, Alleluia: for the Lord God omnipotent reigneth. 7 Let us be glad and rejoice, and give honour to him: for the marriage of the Lamb is come, and his wife hath made herself ready. 8 And to her was granted that she should be arrayed in fine linen, clean and white: for the fine linen is the righteousness of saints. 9 And he saith unto me, Write, Blessed are they which are called unto the marriage supper of the Lamb. And he saith unto me, These are the true sayings of God. 10 And I fell at his feet to worship him. And he said unto me, See thou do it not: I am thy fellowservant, and of thy brethren that have the testimony of Jesus: worship God: for the testimony of Jesus is the spirit of prophecy. 11 And I saw heaven opened, and behold a white horse; and he that sat upon him was called Faithful and True, and in righteousness he doth judge and make war. 12 His eyes were as a flame of fire, and on his head were many crowns; and he had a name written, that no man knew, but he himself. 13 And he was clothed with a vesture dipped in blood: and his name is called The Word of God. 14 And the armies which were in heaven followed him upon white horses, clothed in fine linen, white and clean. 15 And out of his mouth goeth a sharp sword, that with it he should smite the nations: and he shall rule them with a rod of iron: and he treadeth the winepress of the fierceness and wrath of Almighty God. 16 And he hath on his vesture and on his thigh a name written, KING OF KINGS, AND LORD OF LORDS. 17 And I saw an angel standing in the sun; and he cried with a loud voice, saying to all the fowls that fly in the midst of heaven, Come and gather yourselves together unto the supper of the great God; 18 That ye may eat the flesh of kings, and the flesh of captains, and the flesh of mighty men, and the flesh of horses, and of them that sit on them, and the flesh of all men, both free and bond, both small and great. 19 And I saw the beast, and the kings of the earth, and their armies, gathered together to make war against him that sat on the horse, and against his army. 20 And the beast was taken, and with him the false prophet that wrought miracles before him, with which he deceived them that had received the mark of the beast, and them that worshipped his image. These both were cast alive into a lake of fire burning with brimstone. 21 And the remnant were slain with the sword of him that sat upon the horse, which sword proceeded out of his mouth: and all the fowls were filled with their flesh."

SUMMARY:

In Chapter 1, we saw Christ in the midst of the seven golden candlesticks. In Chapters 2 and 3 we saw the whole church age pass before us. In Chapter 4 the rapture took place, and we saw the seven sealed book, the title deed to the earth, in Chapter 5. The tribulation begins in Chapter 6 with the opening of the first six seals, and we saw that one-fourth of the worlds population dies. Chapter 7 tells us of the one hundred forty-four thousand who will be saved at the middle of the tribulation. Chapter 8 is a pause in heaven, probably half-time, as the seventh seal is opened, revealing the seven trumpet judgments. The first four trumpets take place rapidly and affect the earth. Then we are told that the last three trumpets are also the three woes (Revelation

8:13), and they begin in Chapter 9 as the pit is opened and we have hell on earth. Chapter 10 is about Jesus and the little book. Chapter 11:1-13 tells us about the two witnesses who show up after the rapture and are killed by the Antichrist when Satan is cast out of heaven as we saw in Revelation 12. Revelation 11:14 -19 gives us the seventh trumpet, which consists of the seven vials of Chapters 15 and 16, the wrath of Almighty God poured out! Chapter 12 gives us six thousand years of history concerning Satan's attack on Israel and his attempt to kill Jesus. Chapter 13 gives us the unholy trinity of the devil, and Chapter 14 shows us the firstfruits of the tribulation, the one hundred forty-four thousand saved after seeing the two witnesses ascend back to heaven. Chapter 15 introduced the last seven plagues, the seven vials of God's wrath. Chapters 17 and 18 showed us the fall of religious and political Babylon near the end of the seven years. This leads us to the end of the tribulation. Chapter 19 is the second coming of Christ. There are some other major events that take place in this chapter as well.

LESSONS:

1. The Lord is to be praised. (Revelation 19:1-6)
2. God's judgments are true and just. (Revelation 19:2)
3. The marriage of the church, the bride of Christ, is about to take place. It will happen at the end of the seven year tribulation. (Revelation 19:7-9)
4. We will be sinless in heaven. (Revelation 19:8)
5. The second coming of Christ at the battle of Armageddon takes place. Notice that Jesus is a God of war! (Revelation 19:11)
6. The saved will come with Christ on white horses. (Revelation 19:14)
7. Verse 15 is a reference to the one thousand year reign to follow.
8. Verse 19 tells us that the armies of the whole world gather to fight against Christ, but are no match for Him.
9. It is interesting that in verse 20 the beast and false prophet are cast into the lake of fire. In chapter 20:10 the devil is sent to join them.

PERSONAL APPLICATION:

1. How often do I give God praise?
2. Am I bitter at God for something that He allowed into my life?
3. Am I doing my best to present myself as a chaste bride for Christ?

CLOSING: This ends the period of future history called the seven year tribulation. In chapter 20 we will see the Great White Throne Judgment of the lost, which is the second resurrection. In Chapter 21 we will see a new heaven and a new earth. In Chapter 22 we will see a final plea for man to come to Christ.

REVELATION CHAPTER 20

THEME: GREAT WHITE THRONE JUDGMENT

SUMMARY: In Revelation Chapters 1-3 we saw the entire church age. In Chapters 4-5 we saw the rapture and the seven sealed book in the Father's hand. In Chapters 6-19 we saw Christ take the book out of the Father's hand and loose the seals one at a time. In Chapter 19 verse 11 we saw Christ return after the seven-year tribulation was over. We now come to Chapter 20 which is an account of the Great White Throne Judgment. This chapter deals with the resurrection of the lost, the second resurrection. Remember, the first resurrection is in three stages and is for the saved. The second resurrection is for the lost and takes place here in Chapter 20 after the one thousand year kingdom age.

Revelation 20:1: "And I saw an angel come down from heaven, having the key of the bottomless pit and a great chain in his hand.

2 And he laid hold on the dragon, that old serpent, which is the Devil, and Satan, and bound him a thousand years,

3 And cast him into the bottomless pit, and shut him up, and set a seal upon him, that he should deceive the nations no more, until the thousand years should be fulfilled: and after that he must be loosed a little season.

4 And I saw thrones, and they sat upon them, and judgment was given unto them: and I saw the souls of them that were beheaded for the witness of Jesus, and for the word of God, and which had not worshipped the beast, neither his image, neither had received his mark upon their foreheads, or in their hands; and they lived and reigned with Christ a thousand years.

5 But the rest of the dead lived not again until the thousand years were finished. This is the first resurrection.

6 Blessed and holy is he that hath part in the first resurrection: on such the second death hath no power, but they shall be priests of God and of Christ, and shall reign with him a thousand years.

7 And when the thousand years are expired, Satan shall be loosed out of his prison,

8 And shall go out to deceive the nations which are in the four quarters of the earth, Gog and Magog, to gather them together to battle: the number of whom is as the sand of the sea.

9 And they went up on the breadth of the earth, and compassed the camp of the saints about, and the beloved city: and fire came down from God out of heaven, and devoured them.

10 And the devil that deceived them was cast into the lake of fire and brimstone, where the beast and the false prophet are, and shall be tormented day and night for ever and ever.

11 And I saw a great white throne, and him that sat on it, from whose face the earth and the heaven fled away; and there was found no place for them.

12 And I saw the dead, small and great, stand before God; and the books were opened: and another book was opened, which is the book of life: and the dead were judged out of those things which were written in the books, according to their works.

13 And the sea gave up the dead which were in it; and death and hell delivered up the dead which were in them: and they were judged every man according to their works.

14 And death and hell were cast into the lake of fire. This is the second death.

15 And whosoever was not found written in the book of life was cast into the lake of fire.

LESSONS:

1. Satan is no match for God. (Revelation 20:1-3)

2. Satan has many names which signify his character and craftiness. It would do you well to study him to know how to withstand him. *2 Corinthians 2:11: "Lest Satan should get an advantage of us: for we are not ignorant of his devices."*

Notice the many names given to the Devil that describe his evil character.
1. Abaddon, Apollyon meaning destroyer.
2. Satan meaning accuser. He is called *"accuser of the brethren"* in Revelation 12:10
3. Beelzebub in Matthew 12:24
4. Belial in 2 Corinthians 6:15
5. Dragon in Revelation 12:3
6. Serpent in Revelation 12:9
7. Tempter in Matthew 4:3
8. God of this world in 2 Corinthians 4:4
9. The Wicked One in Matthew 13:19
10. Adversary in 1 Peter 5:8
11. Father of Lies in John 8:44
12. Ruler of darkness in Ephesians 6:12
13. Prince of this world in John 12:31
14. A murderer in John 8:44
15. The Enemy in Matthew 13:39

My friend, can you see the horrible and evil nature of the devil? He hates God and everything that God loves. He wants to destroy your life. The Devil hates God with a passion. To get back at God, he tries to hurt that which God loves, MAN. Don't get me wrong, I am sure he hates us too, but only because of what we stand for. The more like Christ we become, the more he hates us, but it is really God he wants to hurt. The Bible warns us of Satan's wiles: *1Peter 5:8: "Be sober, be vigilant; because your adversary the devil, as a roaring lion, walketh about, seeking whom he may devour."* The Bible tells us to defend ourselves against him.

3. Those that live a life for God are well pleasing to God. (Revelation 20:4)

4. Satan will be loosed again after the one thousand years, will deceive the world again, and then be cast into the lake of fire where the beast and false prophet have been since the one thousand years began. (Revelation 20:7-10)

5. Eternal torment and separation from God is the end of all unbelievers. (Revelation 20:11-15)

6. Hell is the temporary place that all lost go at death. The Lake of Fire is the final place for the unsaved after they are judged according to their works. I believe there are different degrees of suffering for the lost, just as there are different degrees of reward for the saved.

PERSONAL APPLICATION:

1. Do I pray and live like my God is all powerful?
2. Have I studied my enemy, the devil, as a general would his foe?
3. Is my life pleasing to God?

CLOSING: It is most interesting to note that the history of the human race begins and ends with man in a perfect environment, and yet he falls (Garden of Eden and Kingdom Age). The lesson is this: man's heart, not his environment, is the problem. *Jeremiah 17:9: "The heart is deceitful above all things, and desperately wicked: who can know it?"*

REVELATION CHAPTER 21

THEME: A NEW HEAVEN AND A NEW EARTH

SUMMARY:

The seven year tribulation, Daniel's seventieth week recorded in Daniel 9:24-27, has taken place in Revelation Chapters 6-19. In Revelation 19:11, Christ has come back with His saints and has defeated Antichrist at the battle of Armageddon. The Antichrist and false prophet were sent to the lake of fire in Revelation 19:20. Satan was bound and locked in the bottomless pit in Revelation 20:2, and the one thousand year kingdom age began. In Revelation 20:11-15 we saw the awful end of all those who reject Christ. They are brought out of hell, judged, and sent to the lake of fire. Chapter 21 picks up right after the one thousand year kingdom age and the Great White Throne Judgment when John sees a new heaven and a new earth, the "New Jerusalem, coming down from God out of heaven."

Revelation 21:1: "And I saw a new heaven and a new earth: for the first heaven and the first earth were passed away; and there was no more sea. 2 And I John saw the holy city, new Jerusalem, coming down from God out of heaven, prepared as a bride adorned for her husband. 3 And I heard a great voice out of heaven saying, Behold, the tabernacle of God is with men, and he will dwell with them, and they shall be his people, and God himself shall be with them, and be their God. 4 And God shall wipe away all tears from their eyes; and there shall be no more death, neither sorrow, nor crying, neither shall there be any more pain: for the former things are passed away. 5 And he that sat upon the throne said, Behold, I make all things new. And he said unto me, Write: for these words are true and faithful. 6 And he said unto me, It is done. I am Alpha and Omega, the beginning and the end. I will give unto him that is athirst of the fountain of the water of life freely. 7 He that overcometh shall inherit all things; and I will be his God, and he shall be my son. 8 But the fearful, and unbelieving, and the abominable, and murderers, and whoremongers, and sorcerers, and idolaters, and all liars, shall have their part in the lake which burneth with fire and brimstone: which is the second death. 9 And there came unto me one of the seven angels which had the seven vials full of the seven last plagues, and talked with me, saying, Come hither, I will shew thee the bride, the Lamb's wife. 10 And he carried me away in the spirit to a great and high mountain, and shewed me that great city, the holy Jerusalem, descending out of heaven from God,
11 Having the glory of God: and her light was like unto a stone most precious, even like a jasper stone, clear as crystal; 12 And had a wall great and high, and had twelve gates, and at the gates twelve angels, and names written thereon, which are the names of the twelve tribes of the children of Israel: 13 On the east three gates; on the north three gates; on the south three gates; and on the west three gates. 14 And the wall of the city had twelve foundations, and in them the names of the twelve apostles of the Lamb. 15 And he that talked with me had a golden reed to measure the city, and the gates thereof, and the wall thereof. 16 And the city lieth foursquare, and the length is as large as the breadth: and he measured the city with the reed, twelve thousand furlongs. The length and the breadth and the height of it are equal. 17 And he measured the wall thereof, an hundred and forty and four cubits, according to the measure of a man, that is, of the angel. 18 And the building of the wall of it was of jasper: and the city was pure gold, like unto clear glass. 19 And the foundations of the wall of the city were garnished with all manner of precious stones. The first foundation was jasper; the second, sapphire; the third, a chalcedony; the fourth, an emerald; 20 The fifth, sardonyx; the sixth, sardius; the seventh, chrysolite; the eighth, beryl; the ninth, a topaz; the tenth, a chrysoprasus; the eleventh, a jacinth; the twelfth, an amethyst. 21 And the twelve gates were twelve pearls; every several gate was of one pearl: and the street of the city was pure gold, as it were transparent glass. 22 And I saw no temple therein: for the Lord God Almighty and the Lamb are the

temple of it. 23 And the city had no need of the sun, neither of the moon, to shine in it: for the glory of God did lighten it, and the Lamb is the light thereof. 24 And the nations of them which are saved shall walk in the light of it: and the kings of the earth do bring their glory and honour into it. 25 And the gates of it shall not be shut at all by day: for there shall be no night there. 26 And they shall bring the glory and honour of the nations into it. 27 And there shall in no wise enter into it any thing that defileth, neither whatsoever worketh abomination, or maketh a lie: but they which are written in the Lamb's book of life."

LESSONS:

1. Revelation 21 takes place one thousand years after the second coming of Christ in Revelation 19:11.

2. Notice in Revelation 21:11-15 that there will be different degrees of punishment. Why else would God bother to judge according to their works?

3. Only lost people stand at this judgment, the second resurrection. (Revelation 20:6)

4. It is believed that the saved will be spectators at the Great White Throne Judgment. This may be why the tears are wiped away in Revelation 21:4. Can you imagine seeing some of your loved ones stand at this judgment?

5. Rest assured, the problems and heartaches of this life will one day be over. (Revelation 21:1)
Revelation 3:11: "Behold, I come quickly: hold that fast which thou hast, that no man take thy crown."
Revelation 2:25: "But that which ye have already hold fast until I come."
Titus 2:13: "Looking for that blessed hope, and the glorious appearing of the great God and our Saviour Jesus Christ...."

6. God's Word can be trusted above all else. (Revelation 21:5)
See also Psalm 12:5-6, Proverbs 30:5, Matthew 24:35

7. Over comers enjoy a unique relationship with the Lord. (Revelation 21:7)
We overcome in three ways according to Revelation 12:11:
   1. By the Blood of the Lamb ....Salvation
   2. By the word of our testimony ....Soul winning
   3. By not loving our lives ....Surrender and sacrifice

8. The gates of pearl are symbolic of the great cost of salvation. (Revelation 21:21)

9. Nothing can compare to the splendor of heaven. (Revelation 21:21)

PERSONAL APPLICATION:

1. Will you hear the words "well done, thou good and faithful servant" at the judgment seat of Christ? Just as not all will suffer the same in hell, we will not all be the same in heaven. Revelation 3:10-13   Hebrews 11:32-35   I Corinthians 3:10-16

2. Am I doing my best to win my friends and loved ones to Christ?

3. Am I living by faith in the written Word of God?

4. Am I an over comer? What do others see in my life?

5. Have I expressed my gratitude to God for the suffering Christ paid to redeem my soul?

6. The sorrows of this life can not compare to the glory of the next life.

CLOSING: Praise God, in heaven there will be no sorrow, no sin, no suffering. There will be no taverns, no red light districts, no death, no cancer, no funerals, or pain. There will be no cussing, no mini skirts, no drugs, no hospitals, or funerals. No murders, no thefts, no locks on doors, no smog, no graffiti, no abortions, or childhood diseases. *Revelation 21:27: "And there shall in no wise enter into it any thing that defileth, neither whatsoever worketh abomination, or maketh a lie: but they which are written in the Lamb's book of life."*

REVELATION CHAPTER 22

THEME: GOD'S FINAL PLEA TO COME

Revelation 22:1: "And he shewed me a pure river of water of life, clear as crystal, proceeding out of the throne of God and of the Lamb.
2 In the midst of the street of it, and on either side of the river, was there the tree of life, which bare twelve manner of fruits, and yielded her fruit every month: and the leaves of the tree were for the healing of the nations.
3 And there shall be no more curse: but the throne of God and of the Lamb shall be in it; and his servants shall serve him:
4 And they shall see his face; and his name shall be in their foreheads.
5 And there shall be no night there; and they need no candle, neither light of the sun; for the Lord God giveth them light: and they shall reign for ever and ever.
6 And he said unto me, These sayings are faithful and true: and the Lord God of the holy prophets sent his angel to shew unto his servants the things which must shortly be done.
7 Behold, I come quickly: blessed is he that keepeth the sayings of the prophecy of this book.
8 And I John saw these things, and heard them. And when I had heard and seen, I fell down to worship before the feet of the angel which shewed me these things.
9 Then saith he unto me, See thou do it not: for I am thy fellowservant, and of thy brethren the prophets, and of them which keep the sayings of this book: worship God.
10 And he saith unto me, Seal not the sayings of the prophecy of this book: for the time is at hand.
11 He that is unjust, let him be unjust still: and he which is filthy, let him be filthy still: and he that is righteous, let him be righteous still: and he that is holy, let him be holy still.
12 And, behold, I come quickly; and my reward is with me, to give every man according as his work shall be.
13 I am Alpha and Omega, the beginning and the end, the first and the last.
14 Blessed are they that do his commandments, that they may have right to the tree of life, and may enter in through the gates into the city.
15 For without are dogs, and sorcerers, and whoremongers, and murderers, and idolaters, and whosoever loveth and maketh a lie.
16 I Jesus have sent mine angel to testify unto you these things in the churches. I am the root and the offspring of David, and the bright and morning star.
17 And the Spirit and the bride say, Come. And let him that heareth say, Come. And let him that is athirst come. And whosoever will, let him take the water of life freely.
18 For I testify unto every man that heareth the words of the prophecy of this book, If any man shall add unto these things, God shall add unto him the plagues that are written in this book:
19 And if any man shall take away from the words of the book of this prophecy, God shall take away his part out of the book of life, and out of the holy city, and from the things which are written in this book.
20 He which testifieth these things saith, Surely I come quickly. Amen. Even so, come, Lord Jesus.
21 The grace of our Lord Jesus Christ be with you all. Amen."

SUMMARY:
We now come to the end of the book of Revelation, and the end of the Bible with a final plea for man to come to Christ for salvation.

LESSONS:

1. Chapter 22 actually is a continuation of chapter 21 with a description of the New Jerusalem. (Revelation 22:1-3)

2. Nothing defiled or impure will ever enter this place. (Revelation 21:27-22:3)

3. We will constantly behold the face of Jesus. (Revelation 22:4)

4. We will never be in darkness again. (Revelation 22:5)

5. The Word of God is faithful and true. (Revelation 22:6)

6. Revelation 22:7-21 brings us back to the time before the rapture, to warn us to be born again before it is too late.

7. When Christ comes, He will come quickly. (Revelation 22:7, 12, 20) There will be no time to make a decision for salvation. (See also Revelation 22:11)

8. The Lord Jesus has given pastors to the churches, the responsibility to testify and preach these things to the people. (Revelation 22:16 seems to refer to the angels we saw in Chapters 2 and 3, who are the pastors)

9. One last plea from God to the lost to be saved. (Revelation 22:17)

10. A stern warning to those who would add or subtract to what God has said. (Revelation 22:18-19) (See also Proverbs 30:6, Jeremiah 26:2, and Deuteronomy 4:2)

PERSONAL APPLICATION:

1. Am I fulfilling the will of God for my life?
Part of the reason you and I are left here when we get saved is to win others to Christ.
2. Am I striving to stay clean and pure for the Lord?
3. Do I long to see His face, or will I be ashamed?
4. Do I realize that whatever I plan to be or do for Christ must be done before the rapture?
5. Am I in a good Bible preaching church under the leadership of a man of God?
6. Do I tend to ignore some of the plain teachings of the Scriptures because they would interfere with my life?
7. Do I look forward to His soon coming?

CLOSING: *Revelation 22:20-21: "He which testifieth these things saith, Surely I come quickly. Amen. Even so, come, Lord Jesus. The grace of our Lord Jesus Christ be with you all. Amen."*

WHO CAN BE SAVED AND WHEN

Let me give you some Scriptures and lessons concerning why I believe nobody gets saved until the second half, and those who reject Christ get no second chance during the tribulation.

CONSIDER THESE SCRIPTURES:

1. II Thessalonians 2:1-12 and note especially verses 11 and 12. Compare with Daniel 12:10 and Proverbs 1:24-33 to see that God's patience does wear thin.

2. All believers are gone at the rapture. The Holy Spirit's convicting power is gone with us. There will be nobody to preach the gospel to the people left. See Romans 10:14-17, I Thessalonians 2:4 as well as Acts 8:29-40 and Acts 10:1-48. See also John 6:44, John 14:26 and John 16:8,13 for reference to Holy Spirit conviction.

3. Consider the open rejection by people during the tribulation who refuse to trust Christ. Could it be because they can NOT trust Christ? Revelation 6:15-17 and Revelation 9:17-21. Consider II Thessalonians 2:11-12 in light of this.

4. In Revelation 14:1-4 we see that the one hundred forty-four thousand Jews are the first ones to be saved during the tribulation. They are called the "firstfruits." According to Revelation 11:13 this takes place right at the middle, as the second woe ends in verse 14. Remember, the second woe is the sixth trumpet.

5. Consider also, that everyone on the earth rejoices at the death of God's two witnesses who are killed at the middle of the tribulation in Revelation 11:1-13. Verse 10 makes it clear that ALL on the earth rejoice, not just the lost, as all are lost at this point.

6. Revelation 13:1-8 is clearly speaking of the middle of the tribulation. Compare Revelation 12:6-13 which speaks of Satan being cast out of heaven at the middle of the tribulation which we see in Revelation 9. The "Saints" mentioned in Revelation 13:7 are the one hundred forty-four thousand new converts and the people they win to Christ.

7. Revelation 6:9-11a are the church age saints, while Revelation 6:11b is the tribulation martyrs that we see in Revelation 7:13-14 who are the one hundred forty-four thousand Jews and their converts.

I see nothing in the entire Bible that shows anyone getting saved before the middle of the tribulation where the one hundred forty-four thousand get saved. I believe many people have a false assurance that their lost loved ones will get saved after the rapture so they have quit witnessing to them.

CAN A PERSON BE 100% CERTAIN OF HEAVEN

One of the most important questions in all the world for a person to get answered, is how to know for certain about his eternal destiny. Can a person know for certain that he is going to Heaven? Let me answer that with a question if I may. Would a loving God leave us down here to wonder and worry about our eternal destiny? Would a loving God leave it to chance? No, my friend, God has not left us here to worry and fret about our eternal destiny. He has made a way for every person to be saved and to KNOW they are saved. 2 Peter 3:9 *The Lord is not slack concerning his promise, as some men count slackness; but is longsuffering to us-ward, not willing that any should perish, but that all should come to repentance.*

Let me say here that you CAN be 100% certain of going to Heaven when you die. I chuckle as I think of the young boy who was asked if a person can know He is going to Heaven. The lad replied, "Yes."

"Well, how do you get to Heaven?" the critic asked again with a grin.

To this the boy replied, "Well, sir, you first got to die." The boy had it partly right, you've got to die first, and the truth is we are all going to die and face God one day. (Maybe sooner than any of us thinks.) In this chapter I plan to show you from the Bible that a person CAN be 100% certain of Heaven when he dies, and what we must do to be certain. Ask yourself honestly, do you know 100% for certain that your destination is Heaven when you die? Is there a time or a place in your mind that you remember getting born again? Should God ask you why you deserve to be let into Heaven, would you have a Scriptural answer? Are you unsure as to your eternal destiny? Would you like to be 100% sure about Heaven? Do you wonder what a person must do to get to Heaven? Is it good deeds, church membership, baptism, reformation, or a combination of these? Can a person REALLY be 100% sure of Heaven before he dies? If you are not sure about Heaven, but are honestly searching for the truth, please read on as I not only show you from the Bible that one CAN be 100% sure of Heaven, but I will also show you how you can be 100% sure that Heaven is YOUR eternal destination today! You say, "You don't know me or what I have done." I don't care what you have done; Christ came to save sinners, little sinners, and big sinners. He saved that wicked thief and murderer who was crucified next to Him; He will save you, too, if you will do what the Bible requires for salvation.

As we begin to search the Scriptures together, ask the Lord to speak to you and show you the truth. Tell Him you want to spend eternity in Heaven, open your heart and mind and let God speak to you. Say something like this: "Dear God, I do not have the assurance of eternal life in Heaven. Please speak to my heart and help me to understand what your Word, the Bible, says about it so I can be saved and have 100% assurance of Heaven today, Amen."

I. FIVE MEN WHO WERE 100% SURE OF HEAVEN

1. KING DAVID KNEW WITH 100% CERTAINTY HE WAS GOING TO HEAVEN.

2 Samuel 12:15 And Nathan departed unto his house. And the LORD struck the child that Uriah's wife bare unto David, and it was very sick.

16 David therefore besought God for the child; and David fasted, and went in, and lay all night upon the earth.

17 And the elders of his house arose, and went to him, to raise him up from the earth: but he would not, neither did he eat bread with them.

18 And it came to pass on the seventh day, that the child died. And the servants of David feared to tell him that the child was dead: for they said, Behold, while the child was yet alive, we spake unto him, and he would not hearken unto our voice: how will he then vex himself, if we tell him that the child is dead?

19 But when David saw that his servants whispered, David perceived that the child was dead: therefore David said unto his servants, Is the child dead? And they said, He is dead.

20 Then David arose from the earth, and washed, and anointed himself, and changed his apparel, and came into the house of the LORD, and worshipped: then he came to his own house; and when he required, they set bread before him, and he did eat.

21 Then said his servants unto him, What thing is this that thou hast done? thou didst fast and weep for the child, while it was alive; but when the child was dead, thou didst rise and eat bread.

22 And he said, While the child was yet alive, I fasted and wept: for I said, Who can tell whether GOD will be gracious to me, that the child may live?

23 But now he is dead, wherefore should I fast? can I bring him back again? I shall go to him, but he shall not return to me.

I want you to see here that David had a child who was dying. For seven days he fasted and wept and prayed for the child to be healed, but the child died and went to Heaven as all babies do that die.

Notice what David said in verse 23, "*I shall go to him, but he shall not return to me.*" You see, David had complete comfort and assurance that he would join his child in Heaven one day. He did not say that he hoped to see him, or he might see him, or he wanted to see him. He said, "I shall go to him." He had complete assurance that he was going to Heaven when he died.

2. THE APOSTLE PAUL KNEW WITH 100% CERTAINTY HE WAS GOING TO HEAVEN.

2 Timothy 4:6 For I am now ready to be offered, and the time of my departure is at hand.
7 I have fought a good fight, I have finished my course, I have kept the faith:
8 Henceforth there is laid up for me a crown of righteousness, which the Lord, the righteous judge, shall give me at that day: and not to me only, but unto all them also that love his appearing.

In the above text, Paul is getting ready to be put to death for his preaching of Christ, yet it is plain to see that Paul knew with 100% certainty that he was saved and on his way to Heaven. He said in 2 Corinthians 5:8 concerning saved folks, "*We are confident, I say, and willing rather to be absent from the body, and to be present with the Lord.*" Paul was absolutely sure about where believers go at death.

3. JOB KNEW WITH 100% CERTAINTY HE WAS GOING TO HEAVEN.

Job 19:25 For I know that my redeemer liveth, and that he shall stand at the latter day upon the earth:
26 And though after my skin worms destroy this body, yet in my flesh shall I see God:
27 Whom I shall see for myself, and mine eyes shall behold, and not another; though my reins be consumed within me.

Job knew his Redeemer was alive and well, and that he would see Him after he died.

4. PETER KNEW WITH 100% CERTAINTY HE WAS GOING TO HEAVEN.

Peter says in 1 Peter 1:4-5 *To an inheritance incorruptible, and undefiled, and that fadeth not away, reserved in heaven for you, Who are kept by the power of God through faith unto salvation ready to be revealed in the last time.*

You see, not only did Peter have assurance of Heaven, but he said, "...reserved in heaven for YOU who are kept by the power of God..." Talk about assurance, Peter is saying that we who have put our faith in Christ, not only have the assurance of Heaven, but that we are KEPT saved by God's power not ours! Now, friend, that is what you call being eternally secure!

5. JOHN KNEW WITH 100% CERTAINTY HE WAS GOING TO HEAVEN.

Read 1 John 5:13. *These things have I written unto you that believe on the name of the Son of God; that ye may know that ye have eternal life, and that ye may believe on the name of the Son of God.*

This is the man called John the beloved. "*The apostle whom Jesus loved.*" John wrote the Gospel of John, first, 2nd, and 3rd John, as well as the book of the Revelation. John knew with 100% certainty he had eternal life, and said that the Scriptures were given so that all believers can "*Know that ye have eternal life.*"

Now I have given you five of the many examples of men in the Bible who knew with 100% certainty that they were saved and going to Heaven when they died. These are folks just like us. "*God is no respecter of persons.*" He does not love one more than another. Let me point out some things these men (as well as us today) all had in common.

II. WHAT THESE FIVE MEN HAD IN COMMON.

1. THESE FIVE MEN WERE SINNERS FROM BIRTH.

Romans 3:10 As it is written, There is none righteous, no, not one: Romans 3:23 For all have sinned, and come short of the glory of God; Romans 5:12 Wherefore, as by one man sin entered into the world, and death by sin; and so death passed upon all men, for that all have sinned....

You see, the Bible teaches that we are all born into this world with a serious problem. We are sinners, and sinners are condemned to suffer Hell for all eternity. You say, "I don't want to hear anything about hellfire and damnation." Well, go ahead and throw this book in the trash and listen to all the false teachers and liars out there then. As long as I have breath, I plan to tell people the honest truth of what the Bible teaches. There is a Hell that burns with fire for those who refuse to accept the plan of salvation which God has provided through Christ. This leads me to the second common trait I see in these five men:

2. THESE FIVE MEN WERE UNDER THE CONDEMNATION OF GOD AND DESTINED TO HELL.

Romans 6:23a "For the wages of sin is death..." And this death is the second death, the LAKE OF FIRE we read about in Revelation 20:14. *And death and hell were cast into the lake of fire. This is the second death.*" And *Revelation 21:8 But the fearful,*

83

and unbelieving, and the abominable, and murderers, and whoremongers, and sorcerers, and idolaters, and all liars, shall have their part
in the lake which burneth with fire and brimstone: which is the second death. We read the chilling story of the rich man who died and went to Hell in Luke 16:23. *And in hell he lift up his eyes, being in torments, and seeth Abraham afar off, and Lazarus in his bosom.* He did not go to Hell because he was rich; he went to Hell because he was not saved. There are scores of Scriptures we could look at concerning the truth of a literal, burning Hell. But that is in another chapter. What I want you to grasp is that these five men, as well as every other person born into this world, were sinners, and as such were under the judgment and wrath of God for their sin. John 3:18 *He that believeth on him is not condemned:*

but he that believeth not is condemned already, because he hath not believed in the name of the only begotten Son of God. Every person will die and go to Hell unless he is cleansed in the blood of Jesus Christ. See 1 Peter 1:19.

3. THESE FIVE MEN WERE SINNERS NOT ONLY BY BIRTH, BUT IN THEIR PERSONAL LIVES AS WELL.

Listen, all five of these men were not only born in sin, (Psalm 51:5) but all five of them have many of their personal faults and mistakes and sins recorded in the Bible for all to see. How would you like for God to record some things concerning your past that nobody but you and God know about? If you do not get saved, your sins will be made known to all when the *"Books are Open"* at the Great White Throne judgment in Revelation 20:12-15. Let me give you just a few examples of the sins of some of these five men as recorded in God's Word:

PETER forsook the Lord and fled when Christ was betrayed in the garden. Later he denied he knew Christ and even cussed and swore. DAVID, the *man after God's own heart*, committed adultery with another man's wife, and had her husband, Uriah, killed to try and hide his sin. JOB was chastened by God for his lack of faith and understanding. PAUL was killing Christians before he got saved, and took a Jewish vow that was not biblical after he got saved, shaved his head, and went to Jerusalem after the Holy Spirit warned him not to go. Paul, when testifying of himself, stated that he was *"The Chief of Sinners."* Even JOHN the Beloved forsook Jesus, struggled with doubt, and quit the ministry for a while. You see, these men were not only born sinners, but they sinned throughout their lives just as you and I were born sinners, and you and I have sinned throughout our lives. If you are honest, you know this to be true. We have sinned against a holy God, we are under the condemnation of God, and must pay the penalty of death and Hell for it. But thanks be to God, He made a way for us to escape the judgment of Hell. This leads me to my final common attribute of these five men:

4. THESE FIVE MEN AT SOME POINT IN THEIR LIVES, ALL PUT THEIR FAITH AND TRUST IN CHRIST TO SAVE THEM.

You see, whether you live in the Old Testament, or the New Testament, or during the Great Tribulation to come, salvation is the same. It is through faith and trust in the finished work of Calvary! Salvation is by trusting what Jesus did on the cross as payment for sin. I don't want to take a lot of time to discuss the meaning of Bible dispensations here, but I do want to make plain to you that there is one way to Heaven throughout the whole Bible, and that way is the cross of Christ! Salvation is through belief and trust in the Gospel. The Gospel is defined in 1 Corinthians 15:1. *Moreover, brethren, I declare unto you the gospel which I preached unto you, which also ye have received, and wherein ye stand;*
2 By which also ye are saved, if ye keep in memory what I preached unto you, unless ye have believed in vain. 3 For I delivered unto you first of all that which I also received, how that Christ died for our sins according to the scriptures;
4 And that he was buried, and that he rose again the third day according to the scriptures:

Even many years before Christ, way back in Genesis, *Noah found grace in the eyes of the Lord,* Noah did not go to Heaven because he was good, he went by trusting in the grace of God who provided a Saviour for him. Abraham believed and trusted the Gospel according to Romans 4:1. *What shall we say then that Abraham our father, as pertaining to the flesh, hath found?*
2 For if Abraham were justified by works, he hath whereof to glory; but not before God.
3 For what saith the scripture? Abraham believed God, and it was counted unto him for righteousness.
4 Now to him that worketh is the reward not reckoned of grace, but of debt.
5 But to him that worketh not, but believeth on him that justifieth the ungodly, his faith is counted for righteousness.

The Bible tells us that the Gospel was preached to the Old Testament people as well as unto us. Hebrews 4:2 *For unto us was the gospel preached, as well as unto them: but the word preached did not profit them, not being mixed with faith in them that heard it.* See, they needed faith in the Gospel of Christ to be saved just as we do. There were many Old Testament types that pointed to Christ. The "brazen serpent" of Numbers 21:9 which Jesus said in John 3:14 represented the cross. The Sabbath, the lamb's blood on the door post, the coats of skins for Adam and Eve, and on and on I could go. But these things did not save anyone nor did the keeping of the Law according to Hebrews 10:1-6, but rather were types to help the people understand and believe the Gospel. This is true of our New Testament baptism and communion ordinances. They do not save anyone, but are simply pictures and types of Christ and the Gospel.

The Bible calls it *"The Everlasting Gospel"* in Revelation 14:6. You see, in the Old Testament, people had to trust in the coming Christ to save them. That is what the animal sacrifices and lambs represented or pictured. They had to place their faith in the coming Lamb of God and His personal sacrifice to save them. That is what John the Baptist meant concerning Jesus when he cried out, *"Behold the lamb of God which taketh away the sin of the world."* Jesus, the Messiah that all the lambs pictured, had arrived. It is no different looking forward to Calvary, than it is for us to look back to Calvary. Abraham had placed his faith in the coming Messiah to save him from his

sins, just as Peter, Paul, and every other saved person in the New Testament must place their faith in the Christ who has already gone to the cross and paid the sin debt for us.

III. WHAT THESE FIVE MEN ARE SAYING TO YOU AND ME

1. We are all sinners, both from birth, and by our sinful lives. *Psalm 51:5 Behold, I was shapen in iniquity; and in sin did my mother conceive me. Romans 3:10 As it is written, There is none righteous, no, not one: Romans 3:23 For all have sinned, and come short of the glory of God;*

2. We are all destined to Hell, the Lake of Fire, the second death, if we die in our lost and sinful condition. *Romans 6:23 "...wages of sin is death..." Revelation 20:15 And whosoever was not found written in the book of life was, cast into the lake of fire. Revelation 21:8 But the fearful and unbelieving, and the abominable, and murderers, and whoremongers, and sorcerers, and idolaters, and all liars, shall have their part in the lake which burneth with fire and brimstone: which is the second death.*

Do you see your condition before God? Do you realize that you are guilty before God and that as a sinner, God cannot let you into Heaven? Do you realize that sin must be paid for, and that God sent His own Son to pay for YOUR sin on the cross of Calvary? *John 3:16 For God so loved the world, that he gave his only begotten Son, that whosoever believeth in him should not perish, but have everlasting life.* Do you realize that if you do not choose to trust what Christ did on the cross as payment for your sin that you are choosing to go to Hell and pay on your sin debt for all of eternity?

3. Just as each of these five men made a personal choice, even so you must make a personal choice to trust in Christ to save you from Hell. You must realize that you are lost in your sin and destined for Hell. You must by faith, personally trust Jesus as your sin bearer, and fully trust Him as your personal Saviour. It is a simple act of faith that merits the grace of God. *Ephesians 2:8 For by grace are ye saved through faith; and that not of yourselves: it is the gift of God: 9 Not of works, lest any man should boast.*

You must realize that your good deeds, your good life, or your membership at a church are not the way to Heaven. Those are good works. You must realize that the sacraments, or baptism, or any other good deed can never get your sins washed away. It is trusting by faith in the price that Jesus paid in full on Calvary that saves us, and that is what gives us 100% certainty of Heaven. Do you understand it? When that wicked jailer in Acts 16 asked Paul how to be saved, Paul told him to believe on the Lord Jesus Christ and put his faith in what Christ had done for him. Not just believe in Him, but on Him, as in trusting in. Look at what it says Acts 16:30. *And brought them out, and said, Sirs, what must I do to be saved? 31 And they said, Believe on the Lord Jesus Christ, and thou shalt be saved, and thy house.*

Friend, this man was saved by putting his faith and trust in Jesus. Paul did not give him a list of things to do, or tell the man to quit all his evil deeds, or join some church. He told him to put his faith and trust in Jesus Christ to be saved. Do you see it? Isn't that simple and right from the Word of God? So many theologians and religions have muddied the waters of the Gospel with tradition and opinions!

Would you like to be saved? Simply bow your head right now wherever you are. Tell the Lord that you are a rotten sinner and undeserving of His love. Tell Him you believe Jesus is the Son of God, and you believe He died on the cross and paid the awful debt of sin that you owe, your eternal Hell. Tell Him that you believe He rose from the dead the third day, and by faith, you are right now repenting of your reliance on a church, or baptism, or some man, or good deeds, or sacrament, and are right now trusting the price Jesus paid on Calvary to save you from your sin, and from Hell, and to take you to Heaven when you die. AMEN!

Reciting a prayer will not save you, but if you have sincerely placed your faith and trust in Jesus Christ to save you, you can now say with 100% certainty that you know you are going to Heaven when you die. Praise the Lord and glory to His name.

Please contact me if you have trusted Christ as a result of reading this that I may rejoice with you. I also would like to send you some free information that will help you in your new life in Christ.

MORE FROM GOODWIN PUBLICATIONS
www.heavenboundone.net

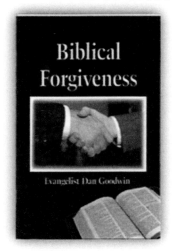

Biblical Forgiveness

The Ten Commandments

A Seven-fold Promise

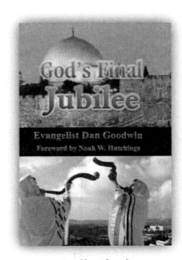

God's Final Jubilee

God's Final Jubilee CD/DVD Set

Times Running Out Gospel Tract